How to Self-Publish Your Book
the CreateSpace Way

**A Step-by-Step Guide
To Writing, Printing and Selling
Your Own Book Using Print On Demand**

Blake Webster

Steve Boga

To symbiotic partnerships everywhere

Contents

Authors' Notes

Section I: A Brief History of Amazon

Section II: A Brief History of POD

Section III: Picking a Topic That Will Sell

Section IV: Starting Your Book

Section V: Keeping the Momentum

Section VI: Making Your Book Shine

Section VII: Laying out Your Book Pages

Section VIII: Amazon Basics

Section IX: Promoting Your Book Online

Section X: Photoshop Primer

Section XI: Conclusion

Section XII: Professional Services

Authors' Notes

Having been an entrepreneur since 1985 and an Internet marketer since 1996, I am always on the lookout for new online ventures that will stand the test of time. That was my mindset when CreateSpace caught my eye.

The concept of self-publishing books for sale in the Amazon catalog first came to my attention in early 2009, when I came across a thread in a webmaster forum, a concept for making money producing and selling books on Amazon. At first I ignored it, as forums are rife with get-rich-quick schemes.

Months later, for some reason I decided to read the thread. It focused on a new way to self-publish on Amazon, called CreateSpace. It was reputed to be a quick and inexpensive way to produce books. Maybe I should give it a try, I thought. I already knew Photoshop, had in fact been working with it every day since 1995. What did I have to lose except time?

In order to test the CreateSpace model, I developed a test book, *Greener Living Today: Forty Ways to a Green Lifestyle*. In writing and publishing that book, I tested every part of the procedure, ordering numerous proofs, learning about search optimization in the book title, making design changes, changing color formats, and editing content.

During all this, I had questions and doubts. Would CreateSpace include a Table of Contents and add page numbers, or would I have to do that? I'd provided my own photographs—how would they look? Would the physical book have the same high quality as those we see on bookstore shelves?

I'm happy to report that CreateSpace books achieve a high standard. In fact, our photos look better than they do in some conventionally published books. And I've consistently been impressed with how easy it is to work with the CreateSpace system and people.

As soon as I saw the first copy of *Greener Living Today*, I knew it was the start, not the end, of my publishing career.

—Blake Webster

*   *   *

As a teacher of weekly memoir-writing classes at the local junior college, I never know who's going to walk through the door—or what impact that person will have on my life. About a year ago, Elaine Webster walked into my class in pursuit of the written word. She found it and stayed.

One day Elaine told me about her husband, Blake. "You two should meet," she said with a wink.

Then we did, at a class Christmas party. Blake, a longtime Internet entrepreneur, told me he was publishing a book, entitled *Greener Living Today: Forty Ways to a Green Lifestyle*. "I hear you're an author," he added.

I told him I'd published more than thirty books, few of which had ever earned me more than my original advance.

He probed further. "You did them all through conventional publishing, right?"

I conceded that point.

"Have you ever heard of CreateSpace . . .?"

And so it went. On that day the seeds of a perfect partnership were planted. I often joke to Blake that between the two of us, we make a complete human being. He, the master of the technical side of the operation; me, the writer of nonfiction books. It's Blake's job to Photoshop the pages, interface with Amazon and CreateSpace, and perform a myriad of other tasks that never brush my consciousness. It's my job to make sure the words are in proper order.

Two years ago, I thought I'd never author another book. CreateSpace and the Webster-Boga partnership changed all that and refueled my ardor for book writing.

No, you never know who's going to walk in the door. Make sure you keep it open.

—Steve Boga

Section I: A Brief History of Amazon

The Origin of Amazon

We see our customers as invited guests to a party, and we are the hosts. It's our job every day to make every important aspect of the customer experience a little bit better.

—Jeff Bezos

Amazon.com, founded by Jeff Bezos, opened for business in July 1995 as an online book vendor. Although sales were immediate, the company made no profit for seven years. Pundits made a cottage industry out of predicting Amazon's demise. Bezos was undaunted. When asked by talkshow host Charlie Rose to describe his outstanding talent, Bezos said it was his focus on the long term and a "willingness to be misunderstood."

Like other successful online companies, Amazon focused on winning the trust and loyalty of its customers. "Our vision," Bezos has often said, "is to be the world's most customer-centric company." In pursuit of that, Amazon began to offer free shipping on orders over twenty-five dollars, a liberal return policy, and credit to customers who discovered the price of a recently purchased item had been reduced—all of which helped Amazon become a household name.

Convenience is another appeal. Sit at your computer with a valid credit card and you can make miracles happen. At least it would have seemed miraculous a few years ago. Place an order in minutes, and it arrives at your doorstep in days. And if you're the type who balks at shipping costs, consider that, according to a recent study, it costs more than fifty cents a mile to drive your car.

Amazon has had a huge impact on retail book sales. There, customers can find books no longer available in bookstores. As of this writing, Amazon has well over 7 million books in its catalogue. In a typical quarter, online vendors—mostly Amazon—sell 2,500 Simon & Schuster titles no longer found in bookstores.

The Kindle

There are two ways to extend a business. Take inventory of what you're good at and extend out from your skills. Or determine what your customers need and work backward, even if it requires learning new skills. Kindle is an example of working backward.

—Jeff Bezos

Amazon has changed the very nature of reading. In 2007, it released the Kindle, an electronic, portable library with a screen that many find surprisingly easy on the eyes. The Kindle allows users to wirelessly download a book in 60 seconds.

Within months after the Kindle's release, publishers saw an exponential leap in sales of their backlist books—those that sell reliably, though often unspectacularly, over time. As of this writing, an estimated three million Kindles are in use, and Amazon lists more than 450,000 e-books. If the same book is available in both paper and paperless, Amazon says, 40 percent of its customers order the electronic version. Amazon also claims that the Kindle has boosted overall book sales. In spring 2010, Russ Grandinetti, an Amazon vice-president, told *The New Yorker* that on average, Kindle users "buy three point one times as many books as they did twelve months ago."

As of May 2010, Amazon.com enjoyed 90 percent of the electronic-book industry's sales. That share will inevitably decline. Apple recently released a Kindle competitor, the I-Pad, and both Sony and Barnes & Noble are creating new platforms to lure e-readers. Fighting back, Amazon has announced plans to release a color version of the Kindle.

Meanwhile, publishers are worried that the low price of digital books will destroy bricks-and-mortar bookstores, which are still their primary customers. Burdened with rent and rising energy costs, they are seldom able to match the discounts offered by online vendors. The results have been predictable, though the numbers still shock. According to the American Booksellers Association, the number of independent booksellers has declined in the past eleven years from 3,250 to 1,400.

Independents now account for just 10 percent of store sales. Chains like Barnes & Noble and Borders cling to about 30 percent of that market; superstores like Costco, Target, and Wal-Mart claim 45 percent, though they carry far fewer titles.

Given these numbers, publishers feel increasing pressure to publish more blockbusters and fewer worthy books on serious subjects. Which brings us to yet another change wrought by Amazon—its impact on self-publishing.

Section II: A Brief History of POD

The First Publishing Revolution: Print on Demand (POD)

When Steve self-published his first book *RISK! An Exploration into the Lives of Athletes on the Edge*, in 1986, digital printing didn't exist. For an initial print run of two thousand books, he had to invest $8,000. Now with Print on Demand (POD) technology, you can publish your book for a few hundred dollars and then order books as you need them.

Print on Demand, sometimes called Publish on Demand, is a printing technology and business process in which new copies of a book are printed when an order is received. POD developed only after the advent of digital printing. Before that it wasn't economical to print single copies using traditional printing technology, such as letterpress and offset printing.

POD publishers generally do not screen submissions prior to publication. They accept uploaded digital content as Microsoft Word documents, text files, or RTF files. Authors choose from a selection of packages, or customize a printing package that meets their needs. For an additional cost, a POD publisher may offer services such as cover design, copyediting, proofreading, and marketing. Some offer ISBN (International Standard Book Numbers) service, which allows a title to be searchable and listed for sale on websites.

Many critics dismiss POD as another type of vanity press. One major difference, however, is that POD publishers have a connection to retail outlets like Amazon.com and BooksInPrint.com that vanity presses generally lack.

Before you commit to a POD publisher, do some comparison shopping. Check out the websites for so-called full-service POD companies, such as Xlibris.com, iUniverse.com, and VirtualBookWorm.com.

Lightning Source and Ingram

One of the first POD book companies was Lightning Source, founded in 1997. Besides offering POD services, Lightning Source operates as a book distributor. It is a subsidiary of Ingram Industries Inc, and a sister company to Ingram Book Group, the largest book wholesaler in the United States.

Every title printed by Lightning Source is included in the Ingram catalog. Even if a book is not physically in Ingram's stock, it can be ordered, printed, and shipped within four hours.

Amazon relies heavily on book title data supplied by both Lightning Source and Ingram, the source for a majority of the titles in the Amazon catalog. Books from Lightning Source and Ingram are usually listed as "in stock," even if Amazon does not have the title on hand.

BookSurge

BookSurge was launched as a POD company in year 2000 by a group of writers committed to developing opportunities for authors both to publish their work and retain content rights and sales profits.

In 2005, Amazon acquired BookSurge and merged it with On-Demand Publishing LLC, an Amazon subsidiary.

In 2008, sales reps from BookSurge informed publishers of POD titles that in order for Amazon to continue selling their POD books, they would have to sign agreements with Amazon's own company BookSurge. Publishers were told that eventually Amazon would carry only POD titles printed by BookSurge.

Although this never came to pass, the threat terrorized publishers and authors, and for about a year they lived in fear that their titles would be pulled from Amazon. It demonstrates the power that Amazon wields in the book industry.

CreateSpace

In July 2005, Amazon purchased CreateSpace.com (formerly CustomFlix), a distributor of on-demand DVDs based in Scotts Valley, California. In 2009, CreateSpace became the dedicated POD platform for all BookSurge and CreateSpace authors and publishers.

CreateSpace represents the second publishing revolution, providing authors with a platform for managing and publishing their work in a creative environment that offers editorial independence, major distribution, the ability to revise content, and a greater share of royalties compared with traditional publishing.

Authors have long been at the mercy of large publishing companies, but now CreateSpace offers a solution that is affordable and fast.

Pro Plan

In December 2009, CreateSpace announced expanded distribution outlets for Pro Plan members. This expanded distribution allows CreateSpace authors/publishers to reach:

1. CreateSpace Direct, which, besides Amazon, includes the CreateSpace eStore.

2. Online bookstores and retailers, such as Ingram and Barnes & Noble.

3. Libraries and academic institutions.

Section III: Picking a Topic That Will Sell

Find Your Niche

I couldn't wait for success, so I went ahead without it.

—Jonathan Winters

When choosing a topic you think will sell, start with intuition and add research. Begin each morning at Google Hot Trends: http://www.google.com/trends/hottrends. Google lists, by date, the most common keyword searches. This listing of top-twenty information requests flags those people, places, and things currently grabbing the public's attention. It may be an earthquake, a celebrity wedding, or a juicy scandal. It may be the latest technology we can't live without or a new 3-D movie.

Now think about related subjects that might interest the people who typed these queries.

- Earthquake preparedness.

- The perfect wedding.

- The dirt on a celebrity.

- Business/political scandals.

- Bargain hunting.

Next, consider possible titles. How-to titles are especially successful. Here are a few examples derived solely from thoughts inspired by one day's search patterns.

- How to Prepare for an Earthquake.

- How to Stage the Perfect Wedding.

- How to Navigate Online Dating Sites and Find the Perfect Mate.

- How to Make Money Photographing Celebrities.

- How to Protect Yourself from Fraudulent Marketers.

- How to Fight Government and Win.

- How to Separate Junk from Treasures When Buying Collectibles.

Use Clickbank to Identify Popular Trends

Clickbank Marketplace (www.clickbank.com/marketplace.htm) is where affiliate marketers go to select digital products to promote on their websites. It is a valuable resource for tracking sales levels of select categories. The Marketplace lists its most popular trends on the left side of the screen and assigns each topic a Gravity Level. A high Gravity Level is one more indication that your topic may be book worthy.

For example, in the Green Products category, when sorted by popularity, the top product relates to alternative energy and has a gravity level of 340.24, indicating that it is being heavily marketed and earning commissions by the affiliates. Toward the end of the listings you will see products with a gravity of 0.00. This means no commissions have been earned by any of the affiliates promoting that product.

- Betting.

- Business/investing.

- Parenting and family.

- Cooking, food, and wine.

- Sports.

- Travel.

This information, though useful, is not a green light to publish. Other questions to ask and answer include:

- Is the market saturated? This can be a tough call. After all, how many biographies of Elvis have been published? When is that market saturated? Moreover, if nothing has been written on your subject, is that a good sign? Despite your passion, maybe no one cares about the sex lives of moles.

- Can I produce a book that offers unique information? Do you have access to something new, such as journals or photographs? Or perhaps a new slant? Specialized expertise?

- Do I intend to buy Google Adwords to promote my book?

The last question concerns Google's paid advertisements. Those ads display to the right and above the non-paid search results. Google makes those areas available for bid. The more popular the subject the more it costs to advertise. If you choose a specialty niche, especially if it has a low Gravity Level, you will be competing with fewer Adword bids.

Consider the number of times your ads will display and the cost per click when deciding if a paid ad position is worth the expense to promote an obscure or specialty product.

Affiliate marketers utilizing Clickbank tend to promote books sold on Amazon.com. Most of them pull in feeds through the Amazon API (application programming interface), based on categories related to their affiliate theme or review site. These sites automatically pull in new books as they enter the Amazon catalog. If you choose the right topic, your book could have hundreds of websites pointing to your book's Amazon page. This, in addition to Amazon's built-in marketing, will help propel your book's sales.

Section IV: Starting Your Book

Love to Write

*Writing is the only thing that, when I do it,
I don't feel I should be doing something else.*

—Gloria Steinem

Years ago, when Steve was profiling dozens of world-class climbers, cyclists, and runners for magazine articles and books, people frequently asked him what the athletes had in common. His answer was always the same: "They love what they do." Although they have superior skills, it is their joy, their passion, for their sport that makes them great.

That, first and foremost, is what you need to bring to the writing game.

Best-selling author Anne Lamott knows what's important: "You'll find yourself at work on, maybe really into, another book, and once again you figure out that the real payoff is the writing itself, that a day when you've gotten your work done is a good day, that total dedication is the point."

Do you feel like that after a good day at the desk? Something close? Writing is hard enough that if you don't love it, if you would rather be a writer than do the writing, you should reconsider this avocation.

On the other hand, maybe you feel something akin to the love for writing revealed here by author Dorothy West:

"When I was seven, I said to my mother, may I close the door? And she said, yes, but why do you want to close the door? And I said because I want to think. And when I was eleven, I said to my mother, may I lock the door? And she said yes, but why do you want to lock your door? And I said because I want to write."

Know the Basics of Good Writing

I try to leave out the parts that people skip.

—Elmore Leonard

Whether your focus is memoir, essay, fiction, or journalism, the basics of good writing remain the same.

- Good writing is aimed at a specific audience. The writer knows the audience and tailors the work to establish a kinship with her readers. The audience understands her even if they don't always agree with her.

- Good writing is interesting. The writer draws the reader in by his choice of words and ideas, by his ability to tell a ripping good yarn. He holds the reader's attention from beginning to end.

- Good writing is simple and concise. The prose is tight, and ideas are expressed clearly. The writer, through diligent editing, has eliminated all unnecessary words, sentences, and paragraphs.

- Good writing reflects the clear thinking of the author. Poor writing is often the product of murky thinking. A good writer knows what she wants to say, and has examined—and reexamined—the content and organization of her material to make sure she has said it.

- Good writing is fresh. The writing flows smoothly, seamlessly, free of redundancies and clichés.

- Good writing relies on strong imagery. Good writers paint pictures. Descriptions are precise and colorful, stimulating the senses and transporting the reader to the scene the writer has created.

- Good writing features correct grammar, spelling, word usage, and punctuation.

Master Basic Grammar and Punctuation

Grammar is a piano I play by ear. All I know about grammar is its power.

—Joan Didion

Admittedly, some writers never master the mechanics of English. But they are rare and provide no excuse for the rest of us to ignore the nuts and bolts of our language. If a writer's first goal is clarity, then the means to that end is the mastery of grammar, punctuation, and spelling. Ignore them at your peril, for the result is bound to be muddled writing and sinking credibility.

Some wonder if the rules of writing apply anymore in this age of "how r u?" e-mails. Indeed they do. Readers must be able to understand your scribblings quickly, without excessive labor. They shouldn't have to struggle to untangle the meaning, and most won't have the patience to read on if they start to lose that meaning.

Think punctuation isn't important? Meaning can turn on a comma:
   A woman without her man is nothing.

Make two punctuation changes and the meaning makes a seismic shift:

   A woman: without her, man is nothing.

Don't be a Slave to Grammar Software

Be cautious about relying too heavily on computer grammar programs. Consider that Lincoln's Gettysburg Address, regarded as one of the most eloquent pieces of prose ever written, gets a flunking grade from RightWriter, a program that checks grammar, syntax, word usage, sentence length, and other elements.

The program considers the first sentence—"Four score and seven years ago . . ."—too long at 29 words, and suggests it be split into two sentences. And, of course, the phrase "all men are created equal" is criticized because it's in the passive voice.

According to RightWriter, Lincoln's writing "can be made more direct by using the active voice, shorter sentences, fewer weak phrases, and more positive wording."

Resolve to Write Regularly

Writing is easy: All you do is sit staring at a blank sheet of paper until drops of blood form on your forehead.

—Gene Fowler

Somerset Maugham worked 4 hours a day; Aldous Huxley 5 hours; Ernest Hemingway 6 hours; Flaubert 7 hours, Joseph Conrad 8 hours. Stephen King once claimed he worked 363 days a year, taking off only Christmas and his birthday; later he admitted he'd fibbed—he actually worked every day of the year.

But take heart: You can be a writer without making that level of commitment. Aim to write daily; settle for no less than twice a week. If you find you've gone weeks without writing, warning bells should sound. Either they will spur you to sit and write, or not. If so, kudos; if not, time to find a new hobby.

If you decide to stick with it, give yourself every chance to succeed. Develop a routine. In fact, the routine is more important than the production. Even no production is okay. As novelist James Jones advised, "Force yourself to sit four hours at the table. Sometimes you get nothing, but the self-discipline is good for you. Somewhere inside you'll be working."

When I'm sitting at my desk staring out the window, my wife doesn't realize I'm working.

—Herb Caen

Create a Workspace

If I fall asleep with a pen in my hand, don't remove it—
I might be writing in my dreams.

—Danzae Pace

Steve once lived in a converted water tower surrounded
by 200-foot-high redwood trees. One day a visitor, awed
by the serene beauty of the place, remarked, "Anyone
could write here!" That's the kind of space you're looking
for: your creative paradise. Find a place that makes you
feel both comfortable and inspired, a sanctuary. For most,
that means a private desk, ideally in your own room or
office, from which you can banish intruders. For almost
everyone, it means peace and quiet.

Keep in mind, however, that there are no hard-and-fast
rules. Hemingway wrote in crowded Parisian cafes.
Others have written standing up, in bed, even in bathtubs.
Find an environment that encourages you to work.

One drawback of working at home is that distractions lurk
everywhere. It's easy to be diverted by the *New York
Times* crossword puzzle, the sports section, or that
vacuum cleaner that needs fixing.

Here's how one writer described a morning's struggle with
word count: "In order not to write, I cleaned a chainsaw,
tried to train some vines up a trellis, rearranged a stack of
boards in the basement, pondered making a goat harness
for a friend, read the last issue of *Popular Mechanics*, and
sawed four old iron-fence palings into a dozen 12-inch
rods for petunia boxes."

Make Time to Write

It takes a good deal of experience to become natural.

—Willa Cather

"How do I find time to write?"—it's the beginner's lament. Granted, writing, if done properly, is hard work and even professional writers have to overcome excuses for not being on the job.

The two most common reasons people don't write:

▪ You don't love it. You love the idea of being a writer more than doing the writing. Eventually, you will drift to something else—painting, lumberjacking—and for a time that will seem equally romantic. If you find yourself going for weeks without writing, you should question your love for the craft.

▪ Life gets in the way. Maybe it's family or work or other people that lures you from the desk. You love writing, but "where did the week go?" You, my friend, need to develop a schedule.

What schedule you adopt is completely up to you. There are dawn writers, daylight writers, and dusk writers. But all of them, a few lapses aside, stick to a schedule.

Develop a Writing Schedule

Don't make the mistake of thinking you'll write when you feel inspired, when your muse slaps you upside the head. Thomas Edison said that genius is 1 percent inspiration and 99 percent perspiration, and that applies to no pursuit more than writing.

Find your best time to write. Leon Uris was a twilight writer. Are you sharpest in the morning or at night? For our parts, Steve is a morning person while Blake is not. What about your biorhythms? Be honest with yourself and schedule accordingly.

As Dominick Dunne advised, "Set a certain time each day to be your writing time, and nothing—nothing—must interfere with that time. THAT IS YOUR WRITING TIME, in capital letters."

Consider two basic ways you can schedule your writing time:

▪ The Rigid Method. This involves a rigid schedule that you follow diligently. Lay out a grid that covers every block of time in your week.

▪ The Spare-Time Method. This is a more flexible schedule that allows you to set goals for the week and to choose which times and days you will write. With the Spare-Time Method, your goal is not putting in a specific amount of time, but rather producing a specific number of words or pages each day.

All that matters is that you reach that word count. It's still important that you write as often as possible, but when you do the work is up to you.

Each method has its advantages. Choose the one that works best for you.

How to Find 30 Minutes a Day

- Get up thirty minutes early and write before others arise.

- Stay up a half-hour later than usual.

- If you work in an office, eat at your desk and write.

- Stop at the library for thirty minutes on your way home from work.

- Write on the commuter train, bus, or ferry.

- Ask your partner to take care of the kids for a half-hour.

- If you have school-age children, postpone your chores for thirty minutes after they leave for school.

- Manage your time more efficiently. Pay attention to where your discretionary time goes and cut thirty minutes of waste.

- If you still find yourself saying, "I don't have time for writing," ask yourself what you mean by that. Do you need to manage your time more wisely? Or is writing not as important to you as you thought?

Become More Observant

On the outskirts of every agony sits some observant fellow who points.

—Virginia Woolf

As we age, we learn to block out stimuli that might deter or divert us from getting from point A to point B. Though that attitude makes us more efficient, it also means we stop noticing the "little things."

To write at your creative best, you'll need to readjust your mindset and begin allowing your brain to acknowledge and register the details you've been blocking out. It may seem difficult at first, but with practice, a whole new world of inspiration will reveal itself.

Here are some activities to get you started:

Listen

Sit quietly for five minutes a day. Don't talk, don't move; just listen. Force yourself to hear—really hear—the world around you. Become aware of the sounds you ordinarily ignore, like your neighbor's wind chimes or the low hum of your refrigerator. You'll be amazed at all the noises you've been missing.

Observe

Go to a park, a concert, a mall, wherever you can watch people. Or head for the hills to observe flora and fauna. Record what you see, smell, and hear.

Move

Boost your observation skills through movement. Walk around a neighborhood or hike a trail—breathe deeply. Force your heart and muscles to work harder than usual and you'll wind up refreshed, with a renewed sense of what's around you.

Play

When was the last time you did something childlike or playful? As we get older, we tend to distance ourselves from play. This attitude is detrimental to creativity, because the ability to see the world through youthful eyes can open doors. Make opportunities to play, especially outdoors. Observe how it feels to be a kid again, as you connect with a part of yourself that's been buried under decades of adult worry.

Good writers are open, not closed. Tune into your senses and miss nothing.

Commit to Improvement

*Once in seven years I burn all my sermons; for it is a
shame if I cannot write better sermons now than I did
seven years ago.*

—John Wesley

You may be an excellent writer right now, but even so, do
you doubt that if you work hard you will be better in five
years? The point is, you always have growth potential—as
long as you stay open to change. Here are some possible
strategies for improving your game:

- Ask people you trust to read your work. Be prepared
for criticism. Learn from it, even when you don't agree.

- Join a writer's club, which can offer support and constructive criticism.

- Take writing classes. Author Irving Wallace credits a
Berkeley school, The Williams Institute, for his development. Wallace believes the value of writing classes is
that they "stimulate the newcomer to write, they force
him to write, and the better ones help him see what is
right or wrong about what he has written."

- Learn the fundamentals of grammar and punctuation.
[see page 41]

- Read a wide range of good writing. Study the work of
writers who interest you.

▪ Take journalism courses, which teach you to write under pressure and to meet deadlines.

▪ Find or hire a personal editor to critique your work. [see page 69] Few are qualified to do the job. You need someone who has both a command of the language and the temperament to tell you when your work needs . . . work.

▪ Concentrate at first on the free forms of prose, such as letters, diaries, journals, reminiscences, memoirs, or family history. Dismiss the thought of publication at first. You want fluency, not fame.

▪ Learn to use a keyboard.

Sit Down

*The art of writing is the art of applying
the seat of the pants to the seat of the chair.*

—Mary Heaton Vorse

The easiest way to start is just to . . . begin. Sit down with
paper and pen or pencil. Or sit at a keyboard. That's the
way to start—by sitting, prepared, with the tools you
need.

You are more prepared than you realize. You already have
the tools of the trade, the words you will use. Every kind
of writing deals in words, and in English we have nearly a
million at our disposal. (According to the Global
Language Monitor, English adds a new word every 98
minutes.)

But don't worry—you know more than enough to tell your
stories. And words can be changed. Sentences and paragraphs can be deleted. Nothing you write is indelible.
False starts and dead ends are common for even experi-
enced writers.

Gracefully accept what Anne Lamott calls "shitty first
drafts."

Craft Gripping Leads

*The last thing we decide in writing a book
is what to put first.*

—Blaise Pascal

Readers tend to remember the beginning and the ending of what they read (the Laws of Primacy and Recency). But the writer who fails to craft a gripping lead won't have to worry about an ending, for the readers will have abandoned the effort long before. As Elmer Wheeler wrote, "Tell it in the first ten words, or you won't get a chance to use the next ten thousand."

The purpose of the lead is to catch the interest of the reader and to indicate, at least generally, what the reader can expect from here on. Your lead should be accurate, brief, simple, informative, clear, and energetic; it should speak to the reader and provide context. Think of your piece as an inverted pyramid: the most important information is presented first, followed by the second most important, and so on.

Whatever lead you choose for a piece, it must:

- Capture the reader's interest.

- Introduce the subject or problem.

- Move smoothly into the body of your piece.

Common lead types

- State a problem.

- Use an interesting quotation.

- Ask the reader a direct question.

- Offer an interesting or unusual fact.

- Offer an alarming or surprising statistic.

- Relate an anecdote or joke.

- Offer an exaggeration of a common situation.

- Show a problem or conflict characters have.

- Show action, in which a character is doing something related to the problem.

- Start with dialogue in which characters are talking about a problem.

- Create a sense of foreboding, a feeling that something important (the problem) is about to happen.

- Depict a humorous situation.

Leads are flashlights that shine down into the story.

—John McPhee

Example

Here is how Frank McCourt began his best-selling memoir, *Angela's Ashes*. What, if anything, about this lead makes you want to read on?

> *When I look back on my childhood I wonder how I managed to survive at all. It was, of course, a miserable childhood: the happy childhood is hardly worth your while. Worse than the ordinary miserable childhood is the miserable Irish childhood, and worse yet is the miserable Irish Catholic childhood.*

Do the Research

If you steal from one author it's plagiarism;
if you steal from many it's research.

—Wilson Mizner

Even if you're writing your own life story, you won't
know everything. How old was I when I contracted polio?
Mom might know. What was the score of the champion-
ship game? Maybe Coach knows.

Get used to querying people who might have the answers
you need. Email makes that easier than ever. Most people
will be flattered that you asked, especially if they know
the answer. Such exchanges will not only refresh your rec-
ollection but spawn new ideas.

Your quest for accuracy should sometimes send you to the
library or to a search engine. One of Steve's students
wrote about the time her uncle ran a marathon. "Imagine,"
she added, "Uncle Mort, who had never completed
anything in his life, went 25 miles without alcohol once
touching his lips . . ."

That's not bad, except that a marathon is 26 miles and
change. It's certainly no disgrace that the writer didn't
know the exact distance. And she was right not to inter-
rupt the creative flow over such a technical point. But
eventually she needs to recognize her uncertainty and get
it right.

About two seconds on Google ought to do it.

Section V: Keeping the Momentum

Develop New Ideas

I never understand anything until I have written about it.

–Horace Walpole

Ideas are in ready supply. The challenge is to latch onto them and make them work for you. Here are some ways to widen the pipeline of new ideas:

▪ Keep a journal. Review your entries for new ideas. Play around with form, style, character, and viewpoint. These experiments will often shake loose new ideas.

▪ Follow your emotions. What gets you worked up—fiction? nonfiction? airplanes? scuba diving? List the things you really care about. What thrills, infuriates, astounds, terrifies, excites, shocks, disturbs, or embarrasses you? The more strongly or deeply you respond to a subject, the more it means to you, the more you will have to say about it, and the more intensely you will say it.

▪ Be observant. Tune into the obvious, and the not-so-obvious. Change your routine; do things that force you to see the world from new perspectives, as though for the first time, as a child might. Or try to see the world through the eyes of another writer—say, a poet or an historian. Watch a loving or quarreling couple and imagine their conversation from both points of view. Role play, pretending you're the pilot, the soda jerk, the victim, the victor.

> Dr. David Reuben conceived his wildly successful sex manual, *Everything You Always Wanted to Know about Sex but Were Afraid to Ask*, while observing honeymooners in Acapulco. Said Reuben: "I'd see them arrive with this just-married glow. And then, the next morning, they might not even be talking to each other. I realized they were completely unprepared."

- Brainstorm with others. Grapple over ideas with writers, yes, but also with other intelligent, creative people you trust. Afterward, write in your journal and note the new ideas that crop up.

- Read good writing. Peruse newspapers, magazines, books, and the Internet for ideas. Subscribe to writers' magazines. Learn how to skim for important material. Visit libraries, and photocopy relevant material. Start files of clippings from your sources.

- Talk to authorities. If you want to include something in your story about climate change, you better chat it up with scientists. If you plan to set a scene at the Indianapolis Speedway, you better engage with a few drivers and greasy pit-crew guys. When Steve wanted extra information on the intestinal parasite giardia, he contacted the Centers for Disease Control in Atlanta as well as local public-health agencies. As you interview your authorities, be alert to new ideas.

• Freewrite. Write uninhibitedly for 5, 10, or 15 minutes at a time. If you get stuck, write the same word over and over until you unstick. Or insert an ellipsis and write, "What I really want to say is . . ." and go on writing. Keep your hand moving and let your imagination go. Deliberately fantasize. Follow your hunches and intuition. Stretch your mind. Lose control and forget about grammar and punctuation. Find your wild mind, and watch the ideas flow.

• Mine conversations for material. One writer, after a fight with his wife, raced to his typewriter and wrote out the angry dialogue. And many others have eavesdropped on the conversations of strangers and used the material in their work.

• Talk with people, particularly people outside of your usual circle. Get them to tell you about their jobs, their childhoods, their families, their values. You may have to prod with specific questions, but in general do more listening than talking. Pay attention not only to what people say, but how they say it.

• Mine other sources for material. Steve's first book, *RISK! An Exploration into the Lives of Athletes on the Edge*, was inspired by a movie entitled *Heart Like A Wheel*, the story of drag-racing champion, Shirley "Cha-Cha" Muldowny. The movie provoked two questions: 1) Why does someone go into an off-beat sport like drag racing? and 2) What skills are necessary to excel? Driven by this curiosity, Steve went on to profile dozens of high-achieving athletes for four books.

- Ask questions. What has always fascinated you? Outer space? The sex life of moles? What would you like to read that hasn't been written? Confirm by perusing *Books in Print*, Amazon.com, and other online retailers.

- Browse through unusual sources. Check out your mother's high school yearbook . . . the Paris Yellow Pages . . . the obituaries.

- Live it up. Experience new places. Travel. Visit a shoelace factory . . . a fishing boat . . . a bocce tournament.

Eliminate Unworkable Ideas

A writer is somebody for whom writing is more difficult than it is for other people.

—Thomas Mann

Steve once put in dozens of hours working on a manuscript about flea markets. Blinded by some amusing stories he'd heard about those events, he thought he could turn them into a book. Then one day it hit him: he doesn't like flea markets.

What he had was not a book, but an idea—and a bad one at that. Bad for him, that is, because his passions lay elsewhere. And that's the point: Follow your passions; do what you love; put the rest aside.

If you catch the writing fever, you will no doubt produce more ideas than you can handle. The challenge then is to eliminate those with the least potential. First, ask some important questions:

- What type of material is it? Is there enough human interest in it?

- Is there a theme to hold it together?

- How important is the idea? Will it influence the groups I'm interested in reaching?

- How original is the idea? Have I read it in other places? Is it just now being talked about?

- How costly and time consuming is the research likely to be?

- Will the material interest me and others for a long time?

- Will the material attract online buyers? [see Section III]

Set Manageable Goals

When I face the desolate impossibility of writing 500 pages, a sick sense of failure falls on me, and I know I can never do it. Then gradually, I write one page and then another. One day's works is all I can permit myself to contemplate.

—John Steinbeck

The title of Anne Lamott's memoir of the writing life, *Bird by Bird*, derives from an incident when she was growing up. Her brother, anguishing over a school project on birds, complained, "There are too many birds." Their father, also a writer, advised, "Just take it bird by bird."

Would-be writers who say "I don't know where to begin" might borrow from Lamott: "Just take it story by story." Don't worry about chronology—you can put the vignettes in order later. Choose an emotional moment from your past and just do the scene. Then do the next one.

Setting out to write a novel-length memoir is much like trying to run a thousand miles. You can't do it at once. But if you run three miles a day, you will reach your goal in a year. So it is with writing. If you aim for a page a day, you will have 365 first-draft pages in a year. Try for 500 words a day; or even 250. As long as you make yourself write every day or so, it won't matter if the word count is low. You will progress. And soon you will become accustomed to setting aside daily writing time.

Learn to Take Criticism

The covers of this book are too far apart.

–Ambrose Bierce

If you're going to get beyond journal writing—that is, take your work public—you're going to have to solicit, and then try to benefit from, criticism. Most of us struggle with the latter and become defensive. But awareness and practice will make you more receptive to constructive criticism.

In Steve's writing classes, the students employ what they call the Rosemary Rule, named after Rosemary Manchester, who has the rare ability to both absorb and deflect criticism. Typically she nods and says pleasantly, "Thanks, I'll think about that."

It's the ideal response, because as author you are final arbiter. Your personal editors can only make suggestions, which you need not heed. Having said that, don't miss the opportunity to learn from the opinions of others. Take criticism as a warning that something is wrong, at least in the eyes of that one critic. When you say, "I'll think about it," really think about it.

But how do you know if what others say has merit? Mystery writer Elizabeth George advises us to "go within," adding:

You can spend your entire life writing and rewriting the same first chapter if you listen to other people's opinions and ignore the one sure place where you will always find the truth: in your own body.

When you are telling the story you are meant to tell, you are actually going to feel the truth of it, and in feeling that truth, your spirits are going to soar. When you are telling that story the way it needs to be told—through the kind of writing you can be proud of—you are going to feel that as well. If you become aware of that feeling of sureness, soundness, and wholeness that develops inside you when you are on the right track, then you won't be led astray by anyone else's opinion.

That doesn't mean you should listen to no one. It means you choose your critics carefully, and when what they say has the ring of truth to it, try it out and see if it feels like truth.

Find a Personal Editor

Some editors are failed writers, but so are most writers.

—T. S. Eliot

Although you must be your own best editor, you also need to show your work to others. More to the point, you must find someone willing and able to read your work with an objective, critical eye. Most people, even your most literate friends, can't help you. Either they will be reluctant to offend or will lack the skills to do so.

Find someone with a critical eye for the language, someone unafraid to speak out, preferably someone who will work for free. Now hang on and don't let go.

Of course, the best editor in the world is wasted on you if you don't learn from her efforts. If she has that key editorial skill—the ability to take a twenty-word sentence, cut eight words, and not lose the meaning—pay attention to that and learn from it. Soon you will be your own best editor, and the editors you do use will wield a scalpel, not a butcher knife.

Remember, everyone needs to be edited.

Break Through Writer's Block

Writing is no trouble: you just jot down ideas as they occur to you. The jotting is simplicity itself—it's the occurring which is difficult.

—Stephen Leacock

Writer's block, when the brain freezes and the fingers cramp into ineffectual claws can drive us to despair. Disturbing questions hound the blocked writer: Is it over? Have I passed my creative peak? Will I ever write again?

Writer's block can strike anybody at any time. What to do?

- Don't panic. You may be afflicted by writer's block in the first place because you are worried, distracted, or depressed. Don't make it worse by dwelling on your inability to write. Failure then becomes a self-fulfilling prophesy.

- Check for external pressures, such as physical or emotional stress, illness, poor diet, inadequate sleep, excessive distractions, or changes or disruptions in your routine. Fix or eliminate as much as possible.

- Change where, when, or how you write. Use pen and paper instead of computer, or write in the early morning instead of at night. Use more or less light; keep a coffee pot going; write in bed or the bathtub.

- Have several different projects going at the same time. When you block on one, put it away and pick up another one. It may be easier to work on a fourth draft of project B than a first draft of project A.

- Work on something other than the lead. Agonizing over a story's lead may be the number-one cause of writer's block. The lead is often the hardest part to write. Even under ideal conditions, you may not be able to write the lead until you've told the rest of the story. But if you're blocked, you should definitely return to it later.

- Stay alert to fresh ideas when you're not blocked. Compile notes and start file folders on possible future projects. Then, when blocked, you have something new to work on.

- Write outside of your usual genre. Writing fiction or poetry can rejuvenate.

- Do a timed freewrite. Even a five- or ten-minute free-write can unclog the pipes.

- Regain the flow by writing letters. Many writers warm up every day by writing letters.

- Focus quietly for a minute or two on the spot where you're stuck. Let your mind wander wherever it wants to roam; such wanderings often lead to something useful.

- Write in your journal. You may even create some-thing—a character sketch, a dialogue—that you can use in one of your stories. If not, at least you've written.

- Keep writing, even if you're seemingly going nowhere. Let the piece wander or lose its way for awhile. If necessary, write nonsense—but keep going. Continue to push ahead until something clicks.

- Look through old photographs. Pictures elicit memories, which can be turned into scenes. You might start by composing captions.

- Brainstorm with other people. Invite and consider fresh perspectives and ideas.

- Meditate and then return to your piece.

- Retype your last page, and then keep right on going.

- Rewrite the troublesome section—this time with a dif-ferent point of view, time, setting, dilemma, or narrator.

- Reward yourself once you finish a project, or a part of a project.

- Go play. See a movie, visit a friend, take a walk. While your conscious mind is off duty, your subcon-scious mind will continue to plug away. Although it's unwise to give in regularly to the voice urging you away from your desk, sometimes a prolonged break can refuel your creative juices. After consulting your doctor, mix exercise into your play.

Even a brisk walk will sharpen attentiveness, reduce stress, and build stamina. You'll write longer and with greater focus.

▪ Get enough sleep. Study after study has confirmed what you already know: insufficient sleep dulls your senses and stunts your creativity.

Become a Capable Interviewer

When people talk, listen completely.
Most people never listen.

–Ernest Hemingway

The interview is at the heart of the writer's research, whether you're writing fiction, memoir, or how-to. Talking to people also gets you out of yourself, increases respect for human differences, and develops your conversational skills.

The first rule is, be conversational. Relax, be friendly and courteous, ask questions. Most people, unless they've been hounded by the press, will take your attention as a compliment and be happy to talk with you. If you are interviewing a friend or family member, all the better.

Some of your answers will come from people you know, and those will likely be easy, informal interviews. But let's say you want to include details about the parasitic worm you got while kayaking the Amazon. You may want to talk to an authority at the Centers for Disease Control; you may have to talk to a stranger.

First and foremost, a good interviewer is a good listener. Pay attention to the answers you get and be prepared to deviate from your script to ask follow-up questions. Although you will get some of your best information from so-called digressions, you may have to gently redirect respondents who roam too far from your line of questioning.

No matter how good a listener you are, you will have to record your subjects' answers on tape or paper. Truman Capote claimed he retained 94 percent of what he heard or read. Few of us approach that figure.

Many interviewers rely on a small tape recorder, which frees you to listen and jot down possible follow-up questions. That leaves the tedious task of transcribing tapes, but at least you know you have the respondent's exact words if you need them.

As a courtesy, ask your subjects if they have any objections to your recording the interview—few will. Finally, make sure your recorder is working and that you have backup batteries. Periodically check the machine to see that it's still running.

Read Good Writing

The man who doesn't read good books has no advantage over the man who can't read them.

—Mark Twain

If you are going to be a writer, you had better be a reader. Reading sharpens your thinking, which in turn sharpens your writing. It awakens you to possibilities and motivates you to write better.

Read everything you can—books, newspapers, magazines, letters, cereal boxes—both for ideas and to immerse yourself in good writing. Always have a book going. Peruse different magazines each week. Subscribe to writers' magazines. Subscribe to at least one newspaper and learn how to skim for important information. Go online and save electronic copies of relevant information, or print them and put them in labeled file folders.

As you read, note what works and what doesn't. Sharpen your eye. Especially analyze the areas in which you struggle—say, dialogue or physical description.

Section VI: Making Your Book Shine

Strive for Clarity

I never understand anything until I've written about it.

–Horace Walpole

The quickest way to lose your readers is through vague or unclear writing. Clarity is the most important quality of tight, interesting writing. No matter how concise your language, how impeccable your spelling and grammar, how gripping your topic—if what you've written isn't clear, you might as well have penned it in Sanskrit.

We're reminded of the importance of clarity when we don't see it, as in this sentence contributed by the Plain English Campaign, an independent group that campaigns against clichés, jargon, and obfuscation: "We are currently experiencing an issue which is impacting the appearance of availability for some seller offerings."

Or in this one: "We are leveraging our messaging leadership to ensure a commercially viable transition path to a high volume, robust and innovative IMS messaging architecture."

If the creator of this masterpiece had shown his work to others, maybe someone would have pointed out that it was unintelligible. But maybe not.

Clear writing starts with clear thinking. William Zinsser cites the president of a major university who wrote a letter to calm the alumni after a bout of campus unrest in the Sixties:

"You are probably aware that we have been experiencing very considerable potentially explosive expressions of dissatisfaction on issues only partially related."

He meant that the students had been hassling them about different things.

Here's another contribution from the Plain English Campaign:

Before: "If there are any points on which you require explanation or further particulars we shall be glad to furnish such additional details as may be required by telephone."

After: "Please call if you have any questions."

Clarity can elude the best of writers. Because we know what we meant to say, we can become blind to creeping ambiguity. But what we meant to say doesn't matter—only what we wrote.

Simplify . . . Simplify

My aim is to put down on paper what I see and what I feel in the best and simplest way.

–Ernest Hemingway

When Steve first sat down to write for publication, his thinking went like this: "I have no experience, no credits, only an above-average vocabulary; so I better use a lot of big words to show it off." And he did—for a while. He once described a merchant in a Bombay [now Mumbai] market as "insouciant." Today he'd be more likely to call her carefree or indifferent—or better yet, show her, through action and dialogue, revealing those qualities.

Don't strive self-consciously for a style. Let your style develop naturally as you learn the craft. The goal, as Nathaniel Hawthorne said, is "to make the words absolutely disappear into the thought."

Emphasize Short Words

"Simplify, simplify," Henry David Thoreau advised us. Unless you're a lawyer or a writer for a scholarly journal, you don't have to dazzle anyone with big words. Beginning writers, especially, must fight the urge to use a 25-cent word when a dime one will do. Legalisms, technical terms and foreign expressions are constantly entering our language—but that doesn't mean you should use them with any regularity. Longer words often look self-conscious and forced. They should be used sparingly, like spice.

Say a character tells another character: "Go to hell!" Or: "I love you." Three little syllables, but what emotional punch they pack. Perhaps you can imagine some powerful two-syllable sentences.

Remember, not all synonyms mean exactly the same thing. Don't say *love* when you mean *infatuation*, but if two words do convey the same meaning, choose the shorter one. Say what you mean in the clearest, cleanest, plainest way you can. Strive to eliminate the fat, the fuzzy, the fatuous, and the fancy. For the most part, shun Latinates like *accomplish* and *purchase* and embrace Anglo-Saxon words like *do* and *buy*.

Exception: If one of your characters tends to pontificate in George Will-like fashion, be faithful to his speech, which may be peppered with Latinates. Similarly, a cop testifying in your courtroom scene will likely say *individual* rather than *person*, and *vehicle* instead of *car*. But when your narrator is speaking to us, keep the language simple.

Example

Change	To	Change	To
accomplish	do	inhabit	live
attempt	try	initial	first
consume	eat	remit	pay
beverage	drink	require	need
demonstrate	show	sufficient	enough
depart	leave	transpire	happen
expenditure	cost		

Be Concise

*The most valuable of all talents is that of
never using two words when one will do.*

–Thomas Jefferson

"Clutter is the disease of American writing," says memoir
maven William Zinsser. Because good writing is concise,
you should strive to eliminate all unnecessary sentences,
phrases, words, even syllables. When in doubt, delete and
see if the passage reads better. If not, you can always
restore it.

Especially scrutinize every adverb. Can you strengthen
the verb and eliminate the modifier? For example: "She
went quickly to the door" would be stronger and more
concise with a better verb: "She darted to the door." Every
time the word very creeps into your prose, a red flag
should unfurl. Look to cut or modify.

Following are common wordy phrases with concise alter-
natives:

Cluttered	Concise	Cluttered	Concise
great in size	great	in relation to	about
twenty in number	twenty	referred to as	called
personal friend	friend	in view of the fact that	as
with regard to	about	with the exception of	except
all of a sudden	suddenly	thought to himself	thought
at the present time	now	until such a time	until
on the subject of	about	prior to the start of	before
completely filled	filled	seems to be	is
during the time that	while	red in color	red
for the purpose of	for	in order to	to

Omit needless words. Vigorous writing is concise. A sentence should contain no unnecessary words, a paragraph no unnecessary sentences, for the same reason that a drawing should have no unnecessary lines and a machine no unnecessary parts.

—William Strunk, Jr.

Pique Our Senses

Some books are to be tasted, others to be swallowed,
and some few to be chewed and digested.

–Francis Bacon

Let's say you're trying to describe the hot, teeming streets
of Calcutta. You want the reader to see the sights, yes, but
also to smell the sweat and smoke and incense, to taste the
curry, to feel the human crush. And so, to make the scene
vivid, you must get beyond sight and describe the setting
in terms of all five senses: sound, smell, taste, touch, and
sight.

If you were describing a circus, you might bring the scene
to life by including the smell of popping popcorn; the
sounds of trumpeting elephants, roaring cats, and calliope
whistles; and the taste of a hot dog.

You add meaning to your sensory description if you let
your characters not merely experience all five senses but
also react to their experience. In the example below, from
Tom Wolfe's bestseller *A Man in Full*, note that the author
does not provide the description, but rather the character
perceives it. It's the difference between "The air smelled
of magnolia" and "Ellen breathed in the scent of
magnolia; it always reminded her of her college days in
North Carolina . . ." The second is personalized. Because
it happens to a character, it is more intimate and immediate, and we care more.

Sensory material will have more meaning for the reader if it means something to one of your characters. The smell of acacia in bloom has greater meaning if someone suffers asthma attacks from acacia.

Finally, you must do all this with light strokes. Most readers will not even notice that you have personalized and unified the story in this way, but they will be drawn into the story by your skills nonetheless.

Example

From *A Man in Full*, by Tom Wolfe

> *As he hobbled on his aluminum crutches toward the Big House, black gnats were dive-bombing his eyes in waves, without any letup. Why the eyes? Probably the water. They wanted to drink the water out of his eyes. Because of his crutches, he couldn't lift his hands high enough to shoo them away. Now he could hear them singing in his ears. In the summertime, South Georgia bowed down helplessly, abjectly, to her rulers, the insects.*
>
> *"That sound," said Serena, "is that the—whuhhhh whuhhhhh whuhhhhh whuhhhh—sound of them eating?"*
>
> *"Yep," said Charlie.*

They did make a sort of crunch crunch sound. In fact, it was the sound of them defecating, the sound of the droppings of tens of thousands of tent caterpillars hitting the ground.

Were your senses piqued? Did you hear those bugs? Feel the irritation? In this same scene Wolff goes on to describe the pungent odor of millipedes crushed on the sidewalk.

Use Strong Verbs

The adjective is the enemy of the noun.

–Voltaire

As your primary tools of persuasion and power, think verbs, not adjectives or adverbs. The verb is the most important word in most sentences, a concept few English teachers mention.

Invigorate your writing by using strong verbs, of which there are many:

build	create	deliver	demand
design	direct	encourage	examine
expand	illustrate	improve	inspect
invigorate	jest	mesmerize	mix
oscillate	persuade	prepare	recommend
repair	retrieve	revitalize	share
shape	simplify	snarl	startle
survey	train	trim	unravel

Avoid Nominalizations. Some writers tend to bury their verbs under nouns and prepositions. Instead of "We discussed . . ." they write, "We held a discussion." The livelier "We agree" is swallowed up by "We are in agreement."

The culprits that aid and abet this smothering are often forms of the verbs to *be, give, have, make,* and *take.* Look out for them in your writing.

Change	To
arrive at a conclusion	conclude
take into consideration	consider
make a determination	determine
make a choice	choose
hold a discussion	discuss
have a suspicion	suspect
have a need	need
be in possession	possess

Avoid Excessive Modifiers. Use a weak verb and you'll be tempted to tack on an adverb, as in: "She went quickly to the door." Because *went* is vague and ineffectual, the author tries to empower it with *quickly*. Best to strengthen the verb itself and drop the modifier. Can you think of a verb that would make the adverb superfluous?

Substitute 'damn' every time you're inclined to write 'very.' Your editor will delete it and the writing will be just as it should be.

–Mark Twain

Show, Don't Tell

Don't tell me the moon is shining; show me the glint of light on broken glass.

—Anton Chekhov

Today's readers, jaded by film and television, are used to "seeing" stories. One reason so many reject novels is that the writer has told a story rather than shown it. The difference between showing and telling is the difference between your characters coming out on stage to act out their roles and a narrator explaining what the characters would have said and done if they could have been here tonight.

How Do Writers Show?

Dialogue is one good way to show. Another is to emphasize verbs. Adjective-noun combinations tend to tell, while verbs tend to show. In the following examples, the first phrase tells, the second begins to show.

loud man . . . man roared

shiny coin . . . coin glinted

old paint . . . paint peeled

sad woman . . . woman wept

happy dog . . . dog wagged tail

Add detail

If you say the dog is happy, you leave it to your readers to fill in the blanks, to decide for themselves how a happy dog looks. But the challenge is to guide your readers through the story. You want to direct, with precision, what they see. The more detail you offer, the more your vision becomes their vision.

> *Steve jammed a sheet of paper into the typewriter. He picked up a pencil, looked at it, and broke it in half. The time for talk was over—he would go see Tom in person.*

Billy is angry, but the reader isn't told he's angry. Instead, the character is given an angry action. Action is a powerful way to show how a character feels.

Note the emergence of showing from telling in the following:

Tells: *She made breakfast.*

Shows a bit: *She cracked two eggs into a bowl.*

Shows more: *As the eggs, sunnyside up, crackled in the frying pan, she hummed her favorite hymn.*

As we move from the general to the specific, the picture we are painting comes into focus. We could continue to add detail and show even more, making the visual come alive with more action. The key to any improvement is specificity.

If you write: "Polly loved to dive in her swimming pool," you are telling, not showing. Information is being conveyed to us; we do not see Polly.

John Updike, however, shows us Polly by painting word-pictures: *"With clumsy jubilance, Polly hurled her body from the rattling board and surfaced grinning through the kelp of her own hair."*

To determine whether you are telling or showing, ask yourself the following questions:

- Are you letting the reader see?

- Is the author/narrator talking at any point?

- Can you silence the narrator by using an action to show what a character feels?

- Is any character telling another character what we already know?

Pitfalls

Beware of three areas where writers are especially likely to tell rather than show:

- When they tell what happened before the story began.

- When they tell what a character looks like.

- When they tell what a characters feels, sees, hears, smells, touches, and tastes.

Paint Word Pictures

*The greatest thing in style is to
have a command of metaphor.*

–Aristotle

Writers use imagery to help readers "see in their mind" as
they read. Imagery is enhanced by specific details (*yellow
tulip* instead of *flower, shrill blast of the horn* instead of
sound) that appeal to one or more of the five senses.

Examples of imagery include alliteration, simile,
metaphor, and onomatopoeia. Although these techniques
can enrich your writing, be careful not to overdo them.

The ability to write strong imagery stems largely from
your powers of observation. Train yourself to tune into
sensual detail. Strive for mindfulness in the here and now.

See Steve's book, *How to Write Your Life Stories:
Memoirs That People Want to Read,* for a more detailed
look at alliteration, simile, metaphor, and onomatopoeia.

Favor the Active Voice

A writer is a person for whom writing is more difficult than it is for other people.

–Thomas Mann

Assertive writing is direct and crisp, unburdened by lifeless verbs, excessive qualifiers, and the passive voice. The voice is active if the subject of the sentence is the "doer." For example: "I bought the book." The active voice is almost always more direct, more economical, and more forceful than the passive.

Passive voice adds words and subtracts clarity. In the passive voice, the subject is acted upon: "The book was bought (by me)." Look for the verb "was" in your writing; it often signals the passive voice.

Sometimes the passive voice is justified—for example, "The Golden Gate Bridge was built during the 1930s." We may not care who built the bridge, only when it was built. But when you use the passive voice sentence after sentence, it's like killing your characters.

One of Steve's students wrote a piece about growing up on a farm in Illinois. Describing the nuts and bolts of farm work, she strung together six straight passive sentences: "The cows were milked . . . The hay was baled . . ." But no one was on stage actually milking or baling; it was just being done. Readers need finely etched characters doing the action, characters they can see and care about.

Examples

Passive: A new safety record was established by me for my department.
Active: I established a new safety record for my department.

Passive: The multiplication tables were learned by Nadia in the fifth grade.
Active: Nadia learned the multiplication tables in the fifth grade.

Passive: In addition, the annual fund-raising dance was coordinated by me.
Active: In addition, I coordinated the fund-raising dance.

Shun Clichés

Never use a metaphor, simile, or other figure
of speech which you are used to seeing in print.

—George Orwell

The first time someone wrote, "Claudius is as fat as a pig," readers probably ooohed and aahed over the rapier-like precision of that simile; today it's a tired cliché.

Clichés are expressions that have been used so much in writing and speaking that they are familiar to readers—too familiar. Clichés make communication stale and boring. Root them out whenever you find them in your writing. Rewrite "quick as a flash," "as plain as day," and "last but not least" as "quickly," "clearly," and "finally." Even better, make the effort and create an original simile or metaphor that eliminates the adverb and turns the sentence into a real gem.

Examples

Unless you are portraying a character prone to uttering banalities, avoid the following expressions—and countless others like them:

- add insult to injury

- green with envy

- in the same boat

- weigh a ton

- on cloud nine

- busy as a bee

- grinning from ear to ear

- white as a ghost

- calm before the storm

- in a jiffy

- at death's door

- not a second too soon

- in this day and age

- heart on her sleeve

- one in a million

Exercise

Choose three clichés, put them in a paragraph, then rewrite them as original expressions.

Root Out Redundancy

*When I see a paragraph shrinking under my eyes,
like a strip of bacon in a skillet, I know I'm on the right
track.*

–Peter de Vries

Steve used to read a book to his daughter, entitled
*Alexander and the Terrible, Horrible No Good Very Bad
Day* (Judith Viorst). That, my friends, is redundancy.

Redundancy comes from a Latin word meaning "to
overflow." In English it means excessive, unnecessary,
wordy, repetitive. When writing term papers for school,
you called it padding. Whatever you call it, get rid of it.
That's what editing is for.

An editor—whether you or someone else—strives to cut
unnecessary words without losing meaning. It's a skill that
can be honed with practice, and by paying close attention
to what good editors do with your prose.

Can you spot any redundancy in this sentence? *I was in
charge throughout the entire project.*

The word *throughout* makes *entire* unnecessary. You
could write: *I was in charge throughout the project.* But
inserting a better verb also improves it: *I remained in
charge of the project.*

Revise . . . Revise . . . Revise

I'm not a very good writer, but I'm an excellent rewriter.

—James Michener

Ernest Hemingway believed "the value of a book can be judged by the value of what is thrown away." And Hemingway threw a lot away. He once confessed that he had rewritten the last page of *Farewell to Arms* thirty-nine times before he was satisfied. "What was it that had you stumped?" asked a journalist. "Getting the words right," he replied.

And when novelist Bernard Malamud said, "I would write a book, or a short story, at least three times: once to understand it, the second time to improve the prose, and a third to compel it to say what it still must say," he was talking only about rewriting, not about the far more numerous editing trips he made through his manuscripts.

Writing is too difficult to expect to get it right the first time. Fortunately, we deal in ink, not oils. Deleting is not only allowed, it's essential. Steve shows no one his work before its time—fifth draft at least. Although many people can write better first drafts than he does, few can craft a first draft superior to his fifth draft.

You must edit . . . then edit some more. If you have the time, put the manuscript away for a week or so, then go through it, now with a more objective, ruthless eye. Take out everything that doesn't belong. Buff what's left until it shines. Repeat as necessary.

Don't be afraid to write crappy first drafts—no one is going to read them. Or rather, no one should read them. All too often, new writers read, show, or submit first or second drafts. It's a habit developed in school, where we first learn to go public with imperfect work.

Yet only after a few drafts does our work begin to glitter. In revision lies excellence. Go find it.

Here's the blueprint, according to novelist Sidney Sheldon:

- Take an idea you really, really like.

- Develop it until it is brilliant.

- Rewrite it for a year or two, until every word shines.

- Then bite your nails, hold your breath, and pray like mad.

In Sum

The two most beautiful words in the English language are "check enclosed."

—Dorothy Parker

A commercially publishable memoir needs at least four elements: large-audience appeal; a sympathetic character or two; a thought-provoking, inspirational story; and good writing. Celina Spiegel, co-editorial director at Riverhead Books, says, "No matter how appealing your story, if you're going to write it down, you have to be able to write."

Here is Steve's Blueprint for Publishing Success.

- Love to write; really love to edit. We don't call the first version a rough draft for nothing. If you craft the perfect metaphor or hit the sweet spot with some dialogue, it's probably during editing. When writing for publication, Steve does at least six drafts. Some authors make more than twenty-five editorial passes.

- Develop a schedule and commit to write regularly. Write several times a week. Standard advice is to write every day, and that's fine if it works for you. But it may be an unrealistic goal. To give yourself every chance to succeed, aim to write three to five times a week. If you find yourself going weeks without writing, it's time to question your commitment to the craft.

- Write nonfiction. About 90 percent of everything published is nonfiction. After you get a few things in print, you can write the Great American Novel.

- Aspire to write well. Join writing groups, devour how-to-write volumes, subscribe to *Writer's Digest*, read voraciously, seek criticism.

- Find a personal editor. Although you need to be your own best editor, you also need to show your work to others. Beware, though, as most people will do little other than crush or inflate your ego—not what you need right now. Mothers are notoriously, sometimes pathologically, supportive, as are many friends. Find someone with a critical eye for the language, someone not afraid to speak out.

- Prepare to compete. Remember, you're doing battle with television, the greatest time-stealer in history, as well as movies, newspapers, video games, the Internet, and countless other distractions. The good news: A market still exists for good stories well told.

- Be interested in the subject you propose. Any insincerity will be revealed in your writing. What's more, you won't have any fun.

- Know your audience. Each article should be directed to a specific audience—veterans, feminists, hockey fans. As you write, picture your readers and tailor the article accordingly.

■ Come up with marketable ideas. Go to *Books in Print* and to Amazon.com and other online resources and find out what has been published on the subject you're considering. When looking for topical topics, visit your local magazine racks and prowl through periodicals. Call publishers or go online and order back copies of the magazines that interest you.

Section VII: Laying out Your Book Pages

Introduction

Real poverty is lack of books.

—Sidonie Gabrielle

Once you've completed your manuscript—including editing, rewriting, and proofreading—it's time to lay out the pages. CreateSpace requires that you submit your pages as an Adobe PDF file, no larger than 100 megabytes (MB). If the file exceeds 100 MB, it will be rejected, as the printing equipment cannot work with files larger than that.

You have a choice of publishing the interior of your book either in black and white or in color. In most cases text will be black, but you may want to include color images or other graphic elements. If you choose color for the interior, CreateSpace will set a minimum price for your book that may be higher than the market will support.

In our first book, *Greener Living Today: Forty Ways to a Greener Lifestyle*, we initially included color photographs inside. The text was conventionally black, but the headers, footers, and inside images appeared in color. Although it's a small book—66 pages—CreateSpace demanded a minimum price of $14.95. We didn't believe the book could command that price tag, so we pulled it from Amazon and converted it to black and white. That allowed us to sell it for $9.95 and still receive a decent royalty.

Color graphics also increase the size of the PDF file. In *Environmentalists in Action,* we included eleven one-eighth-page black and whites. Even those tiny photos made a significant difference in file size, boosting each page from about 400 to 700 kilobytes (KB). In our book *Fountain of Youth,* the pages containing larger photos totaled about 2 MB, whereas text-only pages were closer to 500 KB.

Several desktop publishing programs are available for designing the layout of your book's interior pages, including Adobe Photoshop, Adobe InDesign, and Microsoft Word.

InDesign costs around $800, and Microsoft Word limits your ability to format images and text with precision. For purposes here, we will discuss Photoshop, our preferred method, and a program that many people already own. The tips below are based on the assumption that you know your way around Photoshop. If not, review our Photoshop Primer on page 179.

The Process

▪ First, decide on a book size. Measure the dimensions of books on your shelves to get a sense of it. Our books are trade paperbacks with design dimensions of either 5.25" x 8" or 6" x 9".

▪ Estimate the number of pages. Then go to createspace.com and download a CreateSpace PSD Cover Template from your account dashboard. CreateSpace doesn't provide an interior template, so we use the cover template to set up the interior. We will download another template for the cover when we know the final number of pages.

▪ Crop the cover area to use as a guide for formatting the inside and outside margins. This will eliminate all of the unused white area of your template. The file contains margin guides that show you where you can place content without it being lost in the trimming.

▪ By default, the CreateSpace template has a resolution of 300 DPI (dots per inch). Don't change this, as 300 DPI is mandatory for print quality.

▪ If your book's interior will be printed in black and white, change the Image Mode from RGB to Grayscale. This helps keep the file size low.

▪ Save the template as a new PSD file. I usually assign a filename such as page_master_template1.psd.

• The margin from the spine (distance from the edge of the page to the content area) for a book up to 150 pages can be .25 inches, but .50 inches is ideal. As a guide, turn on the Rulers tool in Photoshop and refer to CreateSpace guidelines.

• Define the text area. Turn on the layer in Photoshop that displays the cropping guides. Here you must decide if you want your pages to contain text only, or if you need to stretch your content by including a header and/or footer on each page. Using headers and footers helps to pad a book that may be light on content. For example, our book, *How to Umpire Baseball and Softball* came in at about 14,000 words; by adding a header and footer to each page, we stretched the content to 104 pages.

• Using the text tool, drag out a text box that fits within your defined area of text placement, then type in some sample text.

• Define your font size and style.

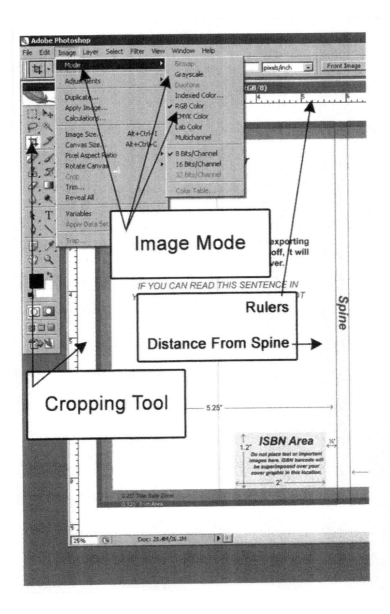

Screenshot #2

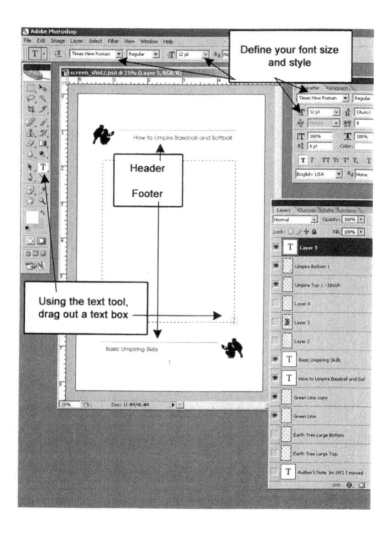

Fonts

Choosing the right font is important for readability and aesthetics. In most cases, you will use a 12-point font. Larger fonts are not recommended unless you want a "large print" or children's book. You might use an 11-point font when you want to insert as much content as possible per page.

Readability and suitability are your chief concerns when choosing your font. Fonts are generally divided into serif and sans-serif designs. Unlike sans-serif, serif fonts have little curlicues on the ends of the letters. For example:

Times Roman is a serif font.

Jaded zombies

Helvetica is a sans-serif font.

Boxer M. Tyson

[Font Samples Courtesy: MyFonts.com]

You can use one of the dozens of free fonts available on your PC, such as Sabon, Garamond, Times New Roman, Helvetica, or Century Schoolbook. If you want a higher-quality font, however, you will usually have to pay for it.

I favor a font called Avant Garde Book. It is commonly used in contemporary designs and advertising. After locating the font, I paid $25 in exchange for a single-user (not single-use) license.

This is an example of Avant Garde Book

If you find a font you like on a website, you can either take a screen capture of that font or scan it and create a jpeg file image. Then go to a site called whatthefont.com, upload the image of the font to that site, and it will give you the status and charges for that font.

Adding Content to the Pages

Once your template is set up, save the file. Then "Save As" the filename of your first page. I typically assign a filename that contains the working title of the book and the page number, such as: "title_of_book_page1".

Now we can begin adding content to the pages. Don't rush this step. Your manuscript must be complete and proofread before laying out the pages. This is important because in Photoshop we will create a new PSD file for each page. Remember to label each file with the corresponding page number.

Our manuscripts are always written in Microsoft Word, so the next step is to start copying the content for each page from Word into Photoshop.

Your text box in Photoshop has been defined in width and height, and this will limit the number of words you can paste on each page. After pasting in your text, delete or add text as necessary.

Once you have finished a page, follow these steps:

1. Save the file. This will allow you to edit the file later if necessary.

2. Flatten the Image (File/Layer/Flatten Image). This will help reduce the file size in the final output to PDF.

3. "Save As" file type PDF File.

4. In the first Dialogue Box, click OK.

5. In the second Dialogue Box, accept all of the default settings except for Compression. To adjust the Compression setting: a) set Compression to JPEG and b) set Image Quality to Medium. As long as the interior of your book is black and white, this will help reduce file size without sacrificing quality. We don't recommend dropping down to the low-medium setting.

You will need to repeat this process for each page of your book.

> Blake likes to keep his PDF files separate from his PSD files, so he creates a separate folder into which he saves the PDF files. This will help later when you consolidate your PDF files into one large PDF file containing all of the pages.

> Remember to label your files with corresponding page numbers in order to identify them.

Images

When selecting interior images, make certain they are 300 DPI in resolution. After pasting them into your Photoshop file, they will automatically convert to Grayscale. Resist the temptation to take screenshots from your computer and include them in your files, because screenshots are captured at only 72 DPI and will not be suitable for print.

Although images enrich your book, they also increase file size. Don't use too many. Remember, you're trying to keep the final file size under 100 megabytes.

If you wish to increase the page count of your book, place images on their own pages instead of inserting them in with the text.

Graphs and Charts

If you build a chart or graph in Photoshop, you have to lay it out line by line and shade it by hand—it's a tedious process.

An alternative is to build your chart or graph in a program such as PowerPoint. When developing your chart or graph in PowerPoint, lay it out as large as possible, then view it in Slideshow mode. At this point, do a screen capture. If your monitor is set at its highest resolution setting, you should capture an image suitable for printing.

Page Order

When laying out the pages of our books, we follow this model:

Page 1: Title (Note: This title has to be identical to a) the title you submit to CreateSpace, and b) the title on the cover of your book. Any deviation and your files will be rejected. This does not apply to the subtitle.)

Page 2: Copyright

Page 3: Dedications or Acknowledgements

Page 4: Blank page

Page 5: Table of Contents

Page 6: Blank page

Page 7: Forward

The first chapter should start on a right-hand (odd-numbered) page. In fact, most sections of a book normally begin on odd-numbered pages.

Compiling the PDF Page Files into One PDF File

Now we need to consolidate all of our PDF page files into a single PDF file. This is the final file that we will upload to CreateSpace.

Many programs are available for consolidating PDF files. We use a free Open Source program for Windows called PDF Split and Merge (PDFSAM) www.pdfsam.org.

You can find the download page here: www.pdfsam.org/?page_id=32.

Instructions:

1. Select Merge/Extract from the navigation column.

2. Locate your PDF files and begin selecting them in small groups in order of page number. If you select all of the files at once, it will load them into the program out of order, and you will then have to painstakingly move each file up or down in the order hierarchy. After selecting each group of files, click OK and they will be added to the program.

3. After you have selected all of your PDF files, save your work as a project by clicking on the "Save" icon located in the upper-left menu bar. Save the project into the same folder where you stashed your PDF files. This will save time later when you're recompiling the PDF files.

4. Make certain you included all of the pages.

5. Choose a destination output and file name.

6. Hit the "Run" button on the lower right to start the compilation.

Screenshot #3

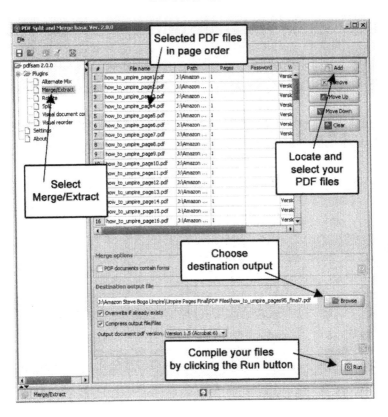

That's it. You now have one PDF file containing all of your pages.

Proofreading

The next step is to proofread your PDF book pages.
Ideally, another person should proof this electronic manuscript, someone removed from the project, someone with
patience and at least a modest command of the language.

Don't skip this step. Typos and other errors will appear in
every book printed. If too many slip through, it will shred
your credibility.

Correcting Mistakes

Correcting mistakes is trivial as long as your PSD page filenames correspond to the actual page numbers, making it easy to identify the files.

Edit each PSD file and repeat the process described above for saving your PDF files.

After editing your files and resaving them as PDF files, go back and recompile the files from your PDFSAM project file.

Laying Out the Cover

Once the interior is finished, you know exactly how many pages your book contains. You need that information before you can lay out the cover.

• Go to CreateSpace and download a new PSD cover template. You will be asked to enter the book's dimensions and number of pages. CreateSpace will then provide you with a PSD file that has the spine width calculated.

• The default settings for the PSD file are 300 DPI and RGB for color. Do not change those settings.

• Crop out the outside white space surrounding the book cover area, then "Save As" a new PSD file. The outside area is not necessary for editing the layout, and eliminating it makes viewing easier.

• The cover file is now ready to work with. At this point, the only layers included are margin guides.

Title

Before you can produce a cover, you have to finalize your title. The length and content of the title will influence other artistic decisions you make about the cover.

Choosing the right title is no trivial matter. In most cases, prospective buyers will see your title before they see your cover. And for maximizing your search-engine presence, your title and subtitle are the most important words you'll create, far more effective than, say, the Description of the book.

Especially for nonfiction, your title should make it clear what your book is about. Since many people read for self-improvement, how-to titles tend to be effective. A book entitled *How to Umpire Baseball and Softball*, as we called our second publication, leaves no doubt about its subject matter.

Subtitle

You are allowed two different subtitles—one that appears on the physical book and an online version strictly for the benefit of search engines.

The main title should include some keywords in it; the online subtitle should be packed with keywords and keyword phrases. Include any keyword or keyword phrase likely to direct people to your book.

Between title and subtitle, you are allowed 200 characters, including spaces, and some authors use the entire allotment. For example, here's an online subtitle that does not appear on the book itself and makes maximum use of keywords:

Free and Cheap Ways to Market, Promote, Advertise, and Increase Traffic to Your Online or Etsy Jewelry Shop and Sell Your Jewelry Now

To achieve a cleaner look, we sometimes choose to eliminate the subtitle from the cover. On the other hand, when we feel a subtitle is necessary to clarify for prospective buyers what the book is about, we include one. With *The Humorous Side of Major League Baseball*, for example, we added just such a clarifying subtitle on the cover:
An Umpire's Look Back at Bizarre Plays, Brawls, Ejections, Funny Stories, Knotty Problems, Tough Calls and More.

Take care to get the title and subtitle just the way you want them. If you decide to change any part of them after submitting the book for review, or after approving the proof, you have to pull the book from Amazon and work with tech support at CreateSpace to make the change. Although there's no charge, the process usually takes about two weeks, during which time your book is off the market.

After we published *The Humorous Side of Major League Baseball*, we realized that we'd neglected to include the keyword *humor* in the title or subtitle. Thus we were excluded from what we thought might be the most common search phrase directing buyers to us: "baseball humor." When you keyed in "baseball humorous," our book topped the list, but that seemed an unlikely way for people to find us. So in spring 2010, we pulled it and added *humor* to the online subtitle.

Basic Cover Design

We favor vibrant covers with plenty of color. A bland, mostly blank cover will fail at its main purpose—to lure buyers. Even when purchasing books online, people still tend to judge a book by its cover. Aim for imagery that catches the eye.

Much of this is subjective, but we favor multi-color covers, sometimes with movement or action, but always depicting a specific theme that runs through the book. When deciding on a cover for our book, *How to Start Your Online Affiliate Store*, we chose a photo of a keyboard. It's a close-up of a dozen or so grey keys; at center stage, an oversized lime-green key labeled "Shopping." Our hope is that the green key says to prospective readers: "Click on me."

For our book, *Environmentalists in Action: Profiles of Green Pioneers*, a collection of interviews with "green" celebrities, we chose a cover shot dominated by the blues and greens of nature. Standing alone on a grassy hillside is a lone tree, which grabs attention.

For the cover of *How to Umpire Baseball and Softball*, we were fortunate to have a great umpire action shot: Steve, arms spread, feet off the ground, making a game-ending safe call at home plate.

Background Color

Your cover image may fill the entire cover, but often it will be cropped and placed on top of a background color. We choose our cover photo first, then pick a background color that blends well with that image.

The cover's background color is a highly subjective decision. Consider your content and themes, and ask: Does a color immediately suggest itself? If you're writing about firemen, you might choose red; a book on nature, green; the Oakland Raiders, silver and black.

If your content suggests no particular color, then you have a decision to make. Consider a range of possibilities. Evaluate book covers in stores and online. Enlist your friends into informal focus groups.

Cover Photo

We normally use a single image, placing it in the center of the cover with the title above and the author's name below. After taking a sample color from the image, we develop a background color for the front and back cover (all one PSD file). This normally generates a cover file size of around 5 MB. For the cover of *Environmentalists in Action*, we used a larger horizontal—or landscape-image and wrapped it around the back cover. That generated a file size of 20 MB, safely under the CreateSpace limit of 40 MB.

Multiple v. Single Cover Photos

For the cover of our first book, *Greener Living Today: Forty Ways to a Greener Lifestyle*, we used five photos, all with an environmental theme. They were pieced together in a puzzle fashion, all with different dimensions. We have vowed never to do it again, if only because it takes so much work. As *Greener Living Today* was a book aimed at testing the CreateSpace model, we wanted to do it for little cost. Since we used Blake's photos, the cover cost nothing. But the process was maddeningly time-consuming, demanding that we crop each image and then fit them all together like a jigsaw puzzle.

In contrast, if you choose a single photo, you simply pop in the image and your cover is done.

Spine Width

Spine text allows us to identify a book sitting upright on a bookshelf. If you want to place text on the spine of your book, CreateSpace recommends that it contain at least 130 pages. However, we tested that limit with *Environmentalists in Action*. It's only 126 pages long, and yet we were able to include spine text. CreateSpace warned us beforehand that the text may not fit neatly on the spine. But four pages is a miniscule width and it came out fine.

Book Length

The minimum number of pages CreateSpace will accept is 24. Maximum file length is 100 MB, so the upper page limit depends on the number of words per page.

The file size for our book, *Fountain of Youth*—with 34,000 words, 185 pages, eight black-and-white photos, and a trim size of 6 x 9—was 90-95 MB. It includes text top to bottom, with no headers or footers. So if your aim is to publish something the length of, say, *Gone with the Wind*, you will have to consider other publishing options—full-service POD companies like IUniverse or XLibris, for example.

Because the first books we published with CreateSpace were quite short, we always chose the *high* compression setting for maximum quality when saving our PDF page files. But when we did that with a longer book, *Fountain of Youth*, the file size swelled to 125 megabytes. We solved the problem by downgrading the Compression setting.

To adjust the Compression setting: a) set Compression to JPEG and b) set Image Quality to Medium. As long as the interior of your book is black and white, this will help reduce file size without sacrificing quality.

Back Cover

When we started writing books the CreateSpace way, we considered putting no content at all on the back cover. After all, we reasoned, these books will seldom appear in bookstores. But when you publish through CreateSpace, your book automatically receives the "Look Inside" feature. That enables people to see the back cover, and we eventually concluded that it too is an important sales tool.

Amazon's Look Inside feature usually takes 10-14 days to implement. If you self-publish without using CreateSpace and you want to activate the Look Inside feature, you must go to Amazon and create an Author Account. There you can arrange to set up the Look Inside feature for any of your books listed on Amazon. You just fill out the forms and Amazon implements it for free.

At your Author Profile page, you can add all of your books to a bibliography list, upload a picture of yourself, and enter a short bio.

When Amazon initially set up Author Profiles, it carried over all the authors listed in the Amazon catalog and established their author accounts. New authors have to apply for an account.

Photoshop the Cover

In Photoshop, you create everything through a series of layers. Each layer is another aspect of the file that can be turned on and off. One layer is background color. Another is the text box into which you copy text, then adjust its placement, boldness, font size and color, and right and left justification. Play around with color and text. This is your chance to be a designer and let your artistic flair come out.

Here are the steps we follow for creating a basic but attractive cover design.

1. Add the first layer and fill it with the color you've chosen for the background.

2. Add a new layer and insert some text in the upper area for a title. Remember, this title must be identical to both the title you submit to CreateSpace and the title on the first page of the book, lest your files be rejected. This does not apply to the subtitle.

3. Add a new layer and insert some text in the lower area for the author's name. If you have something else to promote, consider adding a tagline to your name. With Blake's first book, he added "Publisher of Greener Living Today" after his name because he wanted to promote his online magazine of the same name.

4. Find a dynamic image and insert it into the main area of the cover. We buy our images from iStockphoto (www.istockphoto.com) and Fotolia (www.fotolia.com). Avoid free photos, as you may face copyright issues. Instead, buy them from an authorized source. Plenty of quality shots are available that are inexpensive and royalty-free. Our typical cover photo costs about twenty dollars.

Back Cover:

1. Add a new layer and insert text that briefly but compellingly describes the book.

2. Add a new layer and insert text that describes the author(s).

3. If sufficient space and if warranted, add a quotation, either from an enthusiastic supporter of the book or from someone opining on your subject or theme.

4. Apply the same high standards to your back cover as you do to every other aspect of the book. If the back cover is poorly crafted, prospective buyers will assume it reflects the quality inside.

> If your front-cover photo is a horizontal—or land-scape—format, consider wrapping it around onto the back cover.

Preparing to Submit Your PDF Files

Once your cover work is finished, you need to prepare it for submission to CreateSpace as a PDF file.

1. Save the file.

2. Flatten the Image (File/Layer/Flatten Image). This helps reduce the file size in the final output to PDF.

3. "Save As" file type PDF File.

4. In the first Dialogue Box, hit OK.

5. In the second Dialogue Box, accept all default settings except for Compression. Under the Compression setting, set a) Compression to JPEG and b) Image Quality to High. We want the cover to have the highest quality for print.

Now you have a PDF file that is ready to submit to CreateSpace.

CreateSpace will not accept PDF cover files larger than 40 MB, so avoid using too much imagery. Normally you will be safe using one large image that wraps from the front to back cover, but every graphic element added to the PSD file will boost the final PDF file size. Be careful and adjust the design as necessary.

If you are design challenged, or simply would like an alternative, CreateSpace offers the CreateSpace Cover Creator. It allows you to choose a prefab template design and text content for the front and back cover. The advantages of using the cover creator are convenience and cost. The disadvantage is that you forfeit originality and will probably end up with a design already in use by other books.

Submitting Your PDF Files

Now you've written your book, laid out the pages, and created one PDF file for the interior pages and another for the front and back cover. It's time to go to CreateSpace.com and fill in the fields. To wit:

Field 1: Book title. Remember, the title in this field must precisely match the title on the cover and first page of the book.

Field 2: Subtitle.

Field 3: Description. Provide as much detailed information about the book as you can. This will help potential buyers make the right decision.

> **The Description**. CreateSpace offers a field in which you can include a description of your book. This product description appears on your Amazon book page right below the thumbnail, title, and author bio.

Although there is no word limit, don't ramble. As always, the text will reflect on your writing skills. Try to offer potential buyers a clear sense of what the book is about.

Note: In our experience, the words you choose for your description do little to improve search-engine results.

For example, we edited the description of *The Humorous Side of Major League Baseball*, sprinkling the word *humor* throughout, and it did little or nothing to improve our ranking for the prompt "baseball humor."

Field 4: ISBN number. This is automatically assigned, so you don't have to do—or pay—anything here unless you intend to use your own ISBN, one that you have purchased.

> If you have your own ISBN, you can use it with publishers other than CreateSpace. Your agreement with CreateSpace is nonexclusionary, meaning you're free to take your book to another publisher. But if you've been using an assigned ISBN, you must acquire a new one.

Field 5: The book's category. Choose from a drop-down menu of choices.

Field 6: Country of publication.

Field 7: Publication date.

Field 8: Language.

Field 9: Keywords or keyword phrases. Limit is five.

Field 10: Contributors. List author. If applicable, list co-authors, photographers, illustrators, editors.

Field 11: Author's biography.

Field 12: Physical properties of book, including number of pages. Note: All books have an even number of pages. If you enter an odd number—say, 125 pages—CreateSpace will add a blank page and adjust your entry to 126 pages.

Field 13: The book's interior. Select either black-and-white or color.

Field 14: Trim size—the width and height of the book.

Field 15: Binding. Default is U.S. Trade Paper.

Field 16: Paper color. Select white or beige.

Field 17: Upload your PDF files in two parts. First, upload the PDF for the book's interior. Remember, this file may not exceed 100 MB. Second, upload the PDF for the cover. This file may not exceed 40 MB.

Field 18: Sales channel management. Here you enter the price of your book.

> Setting the price of your book may be more art than science. Still, some standards apply. Set the price of your book too low, and you devalue it in people's eyes. Set it too high and you lose some price-conscious buyers. On the other hand, a higher price tag connotes value and prestige to some—not to mention a higher royalty payout to you.

Try to set a fair and competitive price by researching the prices of similar books. Consider, too, the quality of your work. If it's well written and fulfills its promises, price will be less of an issue.

Royalties are based on more than simply the price of your book. Printing cost is also factored in, and that depends on interior type, trim size, and number of pages.

Our book *Environmentalists in Action*, with black and white interior, a trim size of 5.25 x 8, and 126 pages, has a list price of $14.95. The standard Amazon royalty on the book is $4.98 (33%). Because we signed up for the Pro Plan, our royalty is $6.73 (45%).

Field 19: Enable selling via Amazon.com retail.

Field 20: Enable selling on the CreateSpace store.

Field 21: Here you have the option to purchase Expanded Distribution—aka, the Pro Plan. The price is $40 per year ($5 a year to renew), so you might want to wait on this option until you realize a few sales. With the Pro Plan, your royalty increases and your book appears not only on Amazon and CreateSpace, but also on Barnes & Noble, Ingram, and Baker & Taylor, and is made available to libraries and schools.

CreateSpace Tech Support

If you need help, the tech support people at CreateSpace are remarkably accessible. On your CreateSpace account page, you will see a button labeled "Contact me." When you click on that button, a window pops up. Type in your phone number, click "Call me," and be ready. Your phone will ring immediately. On the other end: a live human being ready to assist you.

We've needed tech support in two major ways: 1) when we changed the interior of *Greener Living Today: Forty Ways to a Greener Lifestyle* from color to black and white, and 2) when we changed the subtitle of *Fountain of Youth*. In both cases, they offered extraordinary customer service.

Section VIII: Amazon Basics

Sales Rankings

*Keep your feet on the ground
and keep reaching for the stars.*

—Casey Kasem

After your book goes live on Amazon, open champagne or whatever, then take a deep breath and prepare to be patient. Evidence suggests that it will take about a year for your title to reach its full sales potential. Of course, there are exceptions. If you've written a book that is timely or falls into a popular niche, you may see immediate sales.

As a book begins to sell, the Amazon sales formula pushes the title higher for various searches, which in turn creates more sales. If your book doesn't sell at first, you might want to purchase the first copy yourself in order to kickstart the sales momentum.

The easiest way to monitor your book's sales is to check its Amazon Sales Rank. Amazon Sales Rank is a measure of how your book rates compared to the other books on Amazon.com. As soon as your book makes its first sale, it acquires sales rank. If your ranking continues to improve—say, from #900,000 to #700,000 to #500,000—it means you are selling books. Sales Rank is updated each hour to reflect recent and historical sales.

You can find sales rank on the book's product page. Scroll down to the section entitled Product Details. Here you will find details about the book, such as number of pages, publisher, even its shipping weight. The last item is Sales Rank.

Here are the Product Details for our book, *How to Start Your Affiliate Store*:

Product Details

Paperback: 78 pages

Publisher: CreateSpace (February 20, 2010)

Language: English

ISBN-10: 1451506708

ISBN-13: 978-1451506709

Product Dimensions: 8 x 5.2 x 0.2 inches

Shipping Weight: 5.1 ounces (**View shipping rates and policies**)

Average Customer Review: 5.0 out of 5 stars See all reviews (**1 customer review**)

Amazon.com Sales Rank: #188,828 in Books (See **Bestsellers in Books**)

With sales updated every hour, the question inevitably arises: How often should I check my Sales Rank? Ultimately that's up to you, but Morris Leventhal of FonerBooks suggests this strategy: List your rank twice a week for four weeks, then add up the numbers and divide by eight. The result is your average Amazon sales rank.

More information on this approach can be found at: **http://www.fonerbooks.com/surfing.htm**.

Checking sales rank more often than twice a week is really meaningless, since one or two sales can temporarily elevate your ranking from, say, #1,000,000 to #100,000. On the other hand, news like that can put a bounce in your step for the rest of the day.

Category Sales Ranks

Although Amazon.com Sales Rank is a good indicator of how well a product is selling overall, it offers few clues about how popular your book is among other similar books. Amazon's Category Sales Ranks were created to highlight books (or other items) that appear in the top 100 in selected categories. Like Amazon's Sales Rank, these category rankings are updated every hour.

For example, one of Steve's early publications, a how-to book entitled *Croquet*, ranks high in one of Amazon's target categories. Go to this link, **http://www.amazon.com/Croquet-Backyard-Games-Steve-Boga/dp/0811724891/**, and at the bottom of the section entitled Product Details, you will see this:

Popular in this category:
#14 in books Sports>Other Team Sports>Cricket

Actual Sales

Amazon generally does not make sales figures available to the public. The company encourages authors to contact their publishers for sales information about their books. If you publish the CreateSpace way, you can view your monthly sales by logging into your CreateSpace account. Then click on the "Sales" link listed to the right of each title in the dashboard; or view a sales report by clicking on the "View Report" link located in the left navigation column. The report breaks down the data into categories, including sales overview, sales by title, sales by channel, sales details, and payment history.

Reviews

Amazon offers a free review service that can be a powerful tool for boosting book sales. Soon after your title goes live on Amazon, secure one or two reviews to jumpstart the sales process.

Start by finding a literate friend who is willing to write a friendly review. Consider offering a free book, but don't demand a five-star review in exchange. We always ask that they read our book and submit an honest opinion. If they can't in good conscience rave about it, we ask that they not write anything at all.

Another approach is to make use of the CreateSpace community forums. Here you can find authors willing to read other authors' books and provide honest feedback. You can access the community forums from your CreateSpace account dashboard.

Click on the link labeled "Community" in the top navigation bar. There you can find opportunities for book reviews under the Books and Marketing and Distribution categories.

Although it's difficult to quantify the impact of reviews, positive ones will certainly help your book sales. Similarly, a bad review can hurt sales. It is disturbingly common for authors, or their agents, to write scathing reviews of their competitors' work. Sometimes competing authors will even post reviews that promote their own title.

In the competitive business world, whether online or not, people sometimes act unethically. Resist the temptation to do likewise. These practices hurt everyone and cast doubt on the entire review process. In extreme cases authors have had customer reviews removed from all of their books.

As detailed in Amazon's General Review Creation Guidelines, Amazon reserves the right to remove reviews that include any of the following:

Objectionable material

1. Obscene or distasteful content.

2. Profanity or spiteful remarks.

Promotional content

1. Advertisements, promotional material or repeated posts that make the same point excessively.

2. Sentiments by or on behalf of a person or company with a financial interest in the product or a directly competing product (including reviews by authors, artists, publishers, manufacturers, or third-party merchants selling the product).

3. Reviews written for any form of compensation other than a free copy of the product.

4. Solicitations for helpful votes.

Inappropriate content

1. Crucial plot elements.

2. Other people's material.

3. Phone numbers, postal mailing addresses, and URLs external to Amazon.com.

4. Details about availability, price, or alternate ordering/shipping.

5. Videos with watermarks.

6. Comments on other reviews visible on the page (because page visibility is subject to change without notice).

Once your book begins to see steady sales, the reviews will develop their own momentum.

Look Inside Feature

If you publish your book through CreateSpace, the Look Inside feature will automatically activate approximately two weeks after your book goes live on Amazon. If you self-publish your book through other means, such as Lightning Source, you can set up the Look Inside feature from your Author Central account. Click on the link in the left column labeled "Allow customers to look and search inside your books."

Author Central

Author Central is a free service provided by Amazon to allow authors to promote their books to more readers. Author Central lets authors share the most up-to-date information about themselves and their work. After creating an account, you can view and edit your bibliography, add a photo and biography to a personal profile, upload book-cover images, and start a blog to connect with readers.

You can also update content in the "Editorial Reviews" section of your books' product pages. The Editorial Reviews section, which appears just above Product Details, allows for five author-added "Review" entries. They include:

- Product Description

- From the Author

- From the Inside Flap

- From the Back Cover

- About the Author

When setting up your title at CreateSpace, the book and author descriptions will appear by default under Editorial Reviews as Product Description and About the Author. You may edit or add content to any of the five entries at any time.

You can sign up and log in to your account at the following address: **https://authorcentral.amazon.com**.

The navigation bar at the top of the page will connect you to areas where you can add your book titles, edit your profile, set up a blog, add videos, and list events.

1. To add books, click on Books/Add more books.

2. To edit your profile, click on Profile/Edit biography.

3. To write a new blog, click on Blog/Create a new post.

4. To add video, click on Videos/Upload video.

5. To add an event, click on Events/Create new event.

You can also add a title to Kindle by clicking on the link in the left column labeled "Publish your content on Kindle."

To add and edit Editorial Reviews, click on the "Book" tab in the navigation bar, and then click on the book title for which you want to add or edit Editorial Reviews. On the detail page, click on "Update the Editorial Reviews." This will take you to the Book Editorial Reviews page, where you can add or edit your reviews.

Kindle

Amazon Kindle is a technological device developed by Amazon.com for the rendering and displaying of e-books and other digital media. Amazon's first hardware device, the Kindle First Generation, was released in the United States on November 19, 2007.

In March 2009, Amazon.com launched an application called Kindle for iPhone, allowing iPhone and iPod Touch owners to read Kindle content on those devices.

With Kindle now available on so many different platforms, you may want to consider adding your book title to the Kindle catalog.

Setting up your title on Kindle is easy; all you need is an Amazon account. Once your account is set up, access Amazon's self-publishing area.

- Scroll to the bottom of any page on Amazon.com and click on "Self-publish with Us."

- In the navigation column on the left, click on "Kindle Books." This will take you to the Digital Text Platform section.

- Click on the "Sign in" button, located on the right side of the page.

- In the upper-left, click on "Add new item" to add your book title.

Here you are asked to provide the following information:

Product Details

- Title.

- Description.

- Author(s).

- Publisher.

- ISBN.

- Language.

- Publication Date.

Confirm Content Rights

- Define territories that you have rights in.

- Confirm that you own all rights.

Upload and Preview Book

Here you will upload an MS Word doc file of your book. PDF files are not accepted.

Note: Kindle will convert all elements in your doc file to the Kindle format. This will assign a default font style and convert any color to black and white.

Enter a Suggested Retail Price

Enable Amazon Kindle Store

Enter the price for the Kindle version of your book.
Kindle pricing varies. Some Kindle versions are priced
the same as the book itself; others are discounted as much
as 50 percent or more. The price you set is a personal call,
but because we don't like creating competition for the sale
of the printed book, we recommend pricing the Kindle
version close to the cover price.

That's it! It usually takes about a week for the Kindle
version of your book to appear in the Amazon catalog.

Search Positioning

Most people search for a book on Amazon by typing in the name of the author, title, or subject. When they type in the subject, or some variation thereof, you want your book to be as close to the top of the listing as possible. Your book's positioning in the Amazon search results correlates to some degree with book sales. But it also correlates with keywords.

If you followed our suggestions and included apt keyword search phrases in your title and subtitle—especially online subtitle—chances improve that your title will display near the top of a search query that relies on those keywords.

To get a sense of how well your title is ranking, type in various keywords in both the Books category and the All Departments category.

For example, when we type "how to write your memoirs" in the Books category, Steve's book, *How to Write Your Life Stories—Memoirs That People Want to Read,* shows up third on the list. In the All Departments category, it appears fourth.

Tags

A tag is a keyword or category label. A concept taken from social networking sites, tags 1) help customers find items on the Amazon site, 2) provide an easy way for customers to classify items for later recall, and 3) supposedly influence Amazon search results and recommendations.

Customers can add tags to a book's product page in an area located just above the Ratings and Reviews section. Customers can also conduct searches via a product's tags. By clicking on a tag, the customer can find related items, discussions, and people.

For example, with Blake's first book, *Greener Living Today*, customers tagged the book with keywords such as *environment, environmentalism, going green ecology, green homes*, and more. Clicking on any of these tags takes you to a page that includes similar books, customers' recommended lists, products, and communities.

The greatest value of a book's tags lies in the number of tags it shares with related book titles. The greater that number, the better the chances that your book will be recommended when those other books are displayed or purchased.

Other Factors

In order to provide the best search results, Amazon's algorithm takes into account the following:

1. Keywords in the title and subtitle.

2. Book purchases resulting from a search.

3. Keyword tags.

4. Sales rank.

5. How often a title is clicked on in search results (click-thru).

6. Keywords within the Look Inside text.

7. Purchases with related titles.

As these factors improve, especially sales rank, purchases, and click-thru popularity, a book title will rise in the search results. As the title moves higher in the search results, these factors are more likely to continue improving as well.

Search results may change slightly on a fairly regular basis, but major changes will occur when Amazon rebuilds the catalog's database, which usually happens twice a week.

Occasionally the rebuild renders out data incorrectly. This might result in your book not displaying in its usual position during a search. No cause for alarm—the problem usually corrects with the next rebuild.

Amazon Recommendations

An extremely powerful feature of the Amazon service is the recommendations it provides customers searching for books and other products.

Amazon determines customer interests by examining the items they've purchased, items they've said they own, and items they've rated. Amazon then compares their activity on its site with that of other customers. Using this comparison, they are able to recommend other items that may interest the customer. You can find these recommended items in several areas throughout the Amazon store.

Recommendations appear on the Amazon home page as "More Items to Consider," "Related to Items You've Viewed," "Inspired by Your Browsing History," and "Customers with Similar Searches Purchased."

Amazon also sends out email recommendations to customers based on their personal shopping habits.

Once your book begins to develop sales momentum, the Amazon recommendation service is just one more application that will help your title develop steady sales.

Section IX: Promoting Your Book Online

Introduction

I have always believed that writing advertisements is the
second most profitable form of writing.
The first, of course, is ransom notes.

—Philip Dusenberry

Once your book is written and published on Amazon, it's time to consider additional measures to spread the word. Developing a website is one effective way of creating exposure and boosting traffic to your book title. Search engine optimization (SEO) will play a key role in determining how successful your website is. Remember, no matter how nice your new site looks, it will serve no purpose if it's not seen.

Here are the best ways to promote your book online.

Use Keywords Wisely

If you followed our instructions for making the best use of keywords in your book title, part of the battle for search positioning has already been won. Google loves Amazon content and spiders the site constantly.

The title of your book also becomes the title of the book's product page, and keywords wisely used there in title tags are one of the best SEO practices available.

Thanks in part to the keywords in our title tags, our book, *How to Start Your Online Affiliate Store*, does well with certain searches. For example, when you type the search query "how to start your online affiliate store," our Amazon product page shows up second out of 19,500,000 results. Change one word—"how to start an online affiliate store"—and we're eighth out of 18,100,000 results. The results are similar at Yahoo.

Another bonus: Affiliate sites that carry the Amazon feed for a book title tend to turn up higher in search results based on that book's title. And CreateSpace eStore listings tend to show up higher in search results than other sites because of their affiliation with Amazon.

We want to apply the same concepts when setting up our promotional website. Make good use of title keywords in the domain name and the title pages of your site.

Design a Website

An excellent way to promote your book is to develop a website devoted to providing information about the book.

Here are some basic guidelines for getting started.

1. Register Your Domain Name

First, you need to register a domain name. We recommend choosing a domain name that contains keywords pertaining to your book title.

For example:

www.makemoneyonlineseries.com
www.howtoumpirebaseball.com

We register all of our domains with GoDaddy, one of the largest registrars, but you can use any registrar you feel comfortable with, such as HostGator or Network Solutions.

2. Find a Hosting Provider

Once you've registered your domain, you need to set it up with a hosting provider. If you have a GoDaddy account, you can use GoDaddy as the provider.

We prefer to use hosting companies that provide *cPanel*, a control panel for the back-end administration of our domains and sites.

GoDaddy is fine, but it can be a little slow and cumbersome when it comes to setting up email accounts and *MySql databases*, a relational database-management system.

We believe HostGator is the best for site setup. A large provider out of Texas, HostGator offers top-notch support, good backup, and a server system that responds quickly to setup procedures.

After choosing your provider, you must change the *name server information* so that the domain points to your new hosting service. If you are using hosting from the same company with which you registered the domain, you probably won't have to change this. Check with the hosting company's technical support.

Name server information will look something like this:

NS1.1111.HOSTGATOR.COM and
NS2.1112.HOSTGATOR.COM

After setting up a hosting account, you will usually be provided with the name server information by email, along with setup instructions.

3 Select a Web Platform

We recommend using WordPress as a content-management system for most sites.

WordPress, an open-source blog-publishing platform powered by PHP and MySQL, can be used for basic content management. It includes many features, including a user-friendly administration panel, a rich plug-in architecture, and an advanced templating system.

Hosting companies offering cPanel will provide you with a "wizard" for setting up WordPress on your new site. Again, HostGator offers excellent technical support if you run into any WordPress installation problems.

When installing WordPress, you will be asked the name of your site. This is where you add the title of your book. It will appear in the title of all your post pages and boost your search-engine positioning.

You can learn more about working with user-friendly WordPress by visiting **www.wordpress.org**.

4. Design a Theme/Template

The next step in your setup is to choose and upload a design for your site.

WordPress is compatible with a variety of themes that will enhance the look and design of your site. Although thousands of themes are free, I tend to gravitate toward higher-quality themes, usually costing $25 to $75. It's your choice. Higher-quality themes are usually better optimized for search engines by making good use of title and header tags (<h1> to <h6> tags are used to define HTML headings), but all WordPress coding is clean and favored by search engines.

To learn more about themes and free downloads, visit the WordPress site at **www.wordpress.org**.

5. Lay Out the Content

We follow a basic formula when organizing and laying out content for a book's site. It consists of creating five posts that contain information about different aspects of the book. Actually, you can create more than five posts, but five is enough for now.

Post One: Title. Besides the title and subtitle, include a description of your book. It doesn't have to be long; in fact, it can be the same description you used when setting up the title at CreateSpace.

Post Two: Preface. This can be the same as the Preface in the book, though if it's quite long, you might want to pull an excerpt. Whatever you do, don't give away too much of the book's main content.

Post Three: Author Bio. This post can contain the same author information you used when setting up the title at CreateSpace.

Post Four: Excerpt from the book. We usually insert an excerpt from the first chapter, but you can use any content that you believe showcases the quality of the book.

Post Five: Buy Now. Include information about the price of the book, along with a link to the Amazon product page.

Get Your Site Indexed Using Backlinks and Pings

Now you want to get your site indexed in Google. Because we use WordPress, we often find our new sites spidered and indexed in Google within twenty-four hours. This is greatly due to the pinging services that WordPress notifies.

Pinging

Update services—Pings—are tools that let other people know you've updated your blog. WordPress automatically notifies popular Update Services, such as Ping-o-Matic, that you've updated your blog by sending a ping each time you create or update a post. In turn, update services process the ping and update their databases with your site's update. The title of your updated content and an excerpt will appear in the update, along with a link back to the post's web address.

Ping lists can be added from your WordPress dashboard. In the left navigation column, select "Settings/Writing." At the bottom of the Writing page there is a field labeled "Update Services." Paste in your list of ping services, and click on the button labeled "Save Changes."

You can obtain a comprehensive Ping list at:
www.prelovac.com/vladimir/wordpress-ping-list.

Backlinking

In addition to Pings, you will want to obtain backlinks from other sites, for indexing purposes and to improve pagerank. Here are two suggestions for effective backlinking:

1. If you have any preexisting sites, or know people who have sites that have age, pagerank, or are regularly spidered by the search engines, add a link to your new site.

2. We have a subscription with USFreeads (**www.usfreeads.com**), and after we set up a new site, we place a classified ad there that contains a link back to the new site. Our ad contains only the title of the site, a description, a price tag of zero, and the web address. Google spiders USFreeads on the hour, so you will see your ad indexed in Google immediately. The Google spider will then follow the link to your site.

RSS Feeds

Another great feature of WordPress is that it produces RSS (Real Simple Syndication) feeds of the content on your site. There are hundreds of RSS feed directories, and other websites will pull the feeds from these directories and display the feed content on their own sites. The feeds contain a link back to the source of the feed, thus providing you with potential traffic and another backlink to your site.

174

We use a program called Traffic Mania RSS Bot, which submits our feeds to about 40 RSS feed directories. You can find out more about RSS Bot at **www.incansoft.com**.

It will help the online promotion of your new site if you build backlinks on a regular basis; however, if you find that you are building backlinks haphazardly, or not at all, consider outsourcing your SEO campaign to a certified SEO consultant.

More tips on backlinking and promoting your site can be found at Basic SEO Direct, **www.basicseodirect.com**.

Adwords

Another way to promote your new book is to make use of Google Adwords. AdWords is Google's flagship advertising product and main source of revenue. AdWords offers pay-per-click (PPC) advertising for both text and banner ads. Google's text advertisements are short, consisting of one title line and two content text lines.

Adwords can be pricey because advertisers bid for ad placement. If your book's niche is highly competitive—say, weight loss or cosmetic surgery—you may want to avoid this approach. On the other hand, if you face little competition, you may be able to purchase advertising for as little as five cents per click.

Make sure the ad's "click thru" URL points to the Amazon product page for your new book.

You can learn more about creating an Adwords account and implementing your advertising campaign by visiting Adwords at **http://adwords.google.com**.

Social Bookmarking Sites

We find backlinking through social bookmarking sites to be a powerful method for obtaining high pagerank and search positioning. Social bookmarking is a way for Internet users to share, organize, search, and manage bookmarks of web resources. Unlike file sharing, the resources themselves aren't shared, merely bookmarks that reference them. Social bookmarking helps search engines find and rank content through links. Backlinking through these sites will help promote traffic to your site, contribute to your link-building campaign, and increase your search-engine rankings.

It may be worth your while to spend a few dollars and obtain thousands of legitimate backlinks. We use a company that provides backlinking through a network of over 350 social bookmarking sites spread over four continents. The process requires submitting your site's RSS feeds to the bookmarking sites. This is yet another benefit of using WordPress, which automatically generates RSS feeds and updates them every time you add new content.

You can find out more about backlinking to social bookmarking sites at Basic SEO Direct, **www.basicseodirect.com**.

Section X: Photoshop Primer

Tutorial for Laying Out the Book Cover

Writing is like prostitution. First you do it for love, and then for a few close friends, and then for money.

—Moliere

In this tutorial we will show you the basic steps for laying out the front and back cover of a book with a trim size of 5.25" x 8".

By following these steps, you will gain a basic understanding of Photoshop and some of its most commonly used tools, especially as they apply to the front and back cover. To learn more about setting up the interior pages of your book, refer to the chapter entitled "Laying out Your Book Pages."

Earlier we described the process for downloading a Photoshop PSD template from CreateSpace. We will begin there, with a downloaded template designed for a book of 126 pages.

Check File Resolution

Print quality requires that a) the working Photoshop file have a resolution of 300 DPI (dots per inch,) and b) the image mode be set for RGB (red, green, blue). These are the default settings in the downloaded template.

To view the settings, open the file in Photoshop; from the top menu select "Image/Image Size." Here you can view the height and width of your document and the resolution.

To view the image mode, select "Image/Mode." Here you should see that RGB is selected.

Screenshot #4

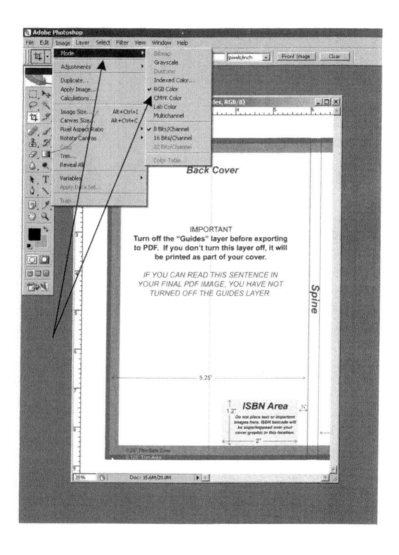

Screenshot #5

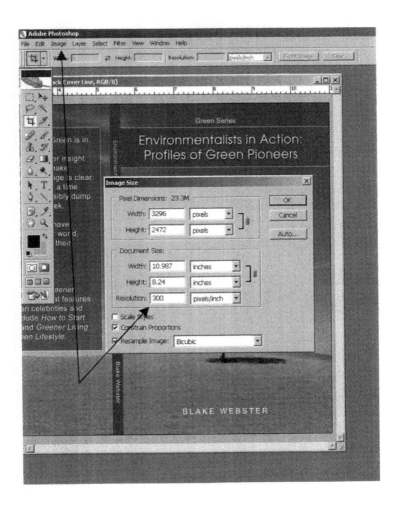

Step One

Crop off the white area surrounding the book cover edges.

Screenshot #6

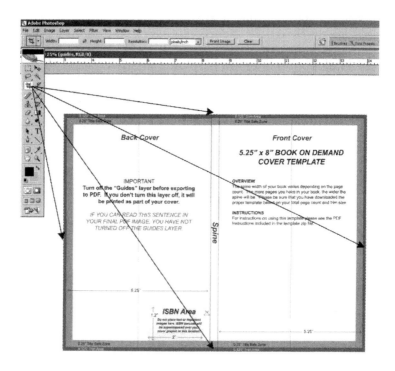

Go to "File/Save As" and save the file as a new PSD file, giving it a new file name.

We tend to use the original file name along with the wording "master1." This results in a file name like this: BookCover5_25X8_BW_120_master1.psd.

Layers

Your template has a white background and a layer that contains the guides for the book trim. The guides indicate areas that will be cut off during printing. This layer also includes a defined area for the spine.

When adding layers to the design, be sure to keep the guide layers at the top of the layer menu. Layers in Photoshop display design elements in a top-to-bottom order. The top layer will always display its content on top of the layer below it.

For example, if the bottom layer contains a solid color and the layer above it contains some text, the text layer will be visible on top of the color. If the color layer is moved (dragged) above the text layer, the text will disappear behind the color layer.

Layers can be turned on and off. If a layer is on, it will save and print as part of the final image. If a layer is turned off, it will not display in the final output.

Screenshot #7

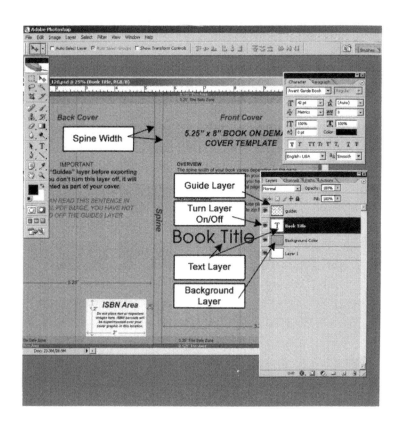

Step Two

Now we choose a background color. We will use the same color for both front and back cover.

1. Add a new layer and assign it a title.

2. Use the color picker to choose a color.

3. Make certain the proper layer is selected, then go to "Edit/Fill/Foreground Color" and fill the layer with the chosen color.

Screenshot #8

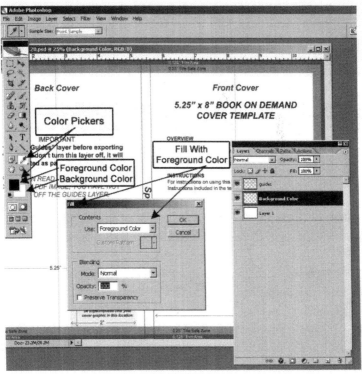

Step Three

Next we will add a color strip across the top, as a background for the title. The strip will be black in color with white lines across the top and bottom. We will extend this strip across the front and back cover.

1. Add a new layer and give it a title.

2. Use the color picker to choose a color.

3. After making certain the proper layer is selected, use the rectangle tool to draw the color strip. Go to "Edit/Fill/Foreground Color" and fill the layer with the chosen color.

4. Add a new layer for the top white line and give it a title.

5. Use the color picker to choose a color.

6. Select the next layer, then use the line tool with the pixels set at 3; draw a line across the top of the color strip. Use the move tool to maneuver the line into position.

7. Make a copy of the top line layer and title the copied layer "bottom line." Use the move tool to maneuver the line into position at the bottom of the color strip.

Screenshot #9

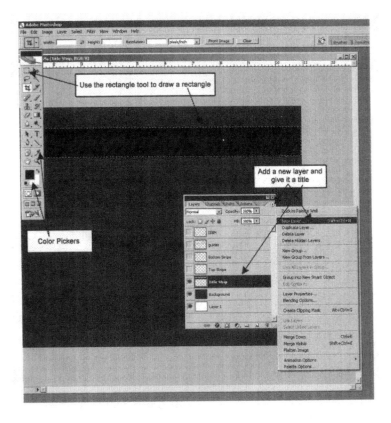

Screenshot #10

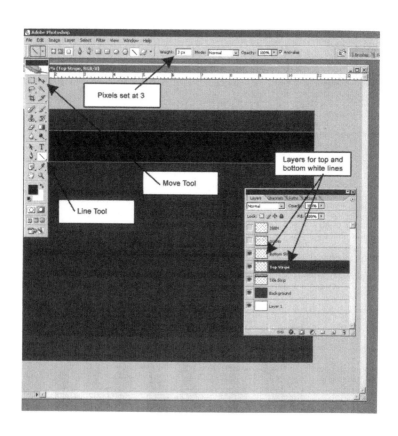

Step Four

Now we will add the title text on top of the color strip layer.

1.   Add a new layer and give it a title.

2.   Select the text tool, and choose a font and color for the title text.

3.   Click on the area over the color strip into which you want to type the text.

4.   Type in the text for the title.

Repeat the above procedure to add the subtitle and author's name to other areas of the cover.

Screenshot #11

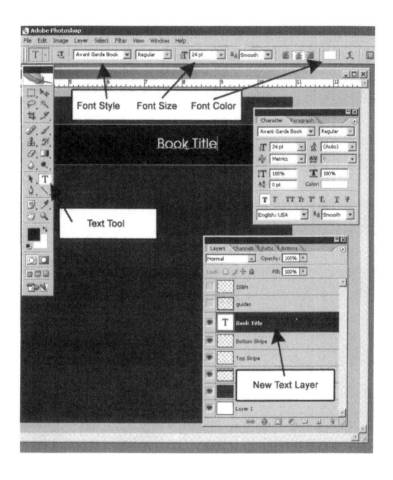

Step Five

Now we add an image to the front cover.

When acquiring images, be sure they have a resolution of 300 DPI. Stock photo outlets vary in the way they describe image resolution, so if you're uncertain, check with the vendor.

1. Open up the image in Photoshop alongside your template.

2. Experiment with resizing the image in order to arrive at the correct dimensions. Try different widths and heights by going to "Image/Image Size." In the properties window, adjust the width and height. Make certain to enable "Constrain Proportions" in order to maintain the aspect ratio of the image.

3. Add a new layer in your template and give it a title.

4. Copy the image: "Edit/Copy."

5. Paste the image into the template: "Edit/Paste."

6. Use the move tool to maneuver the image into position.

7. If the image is too large or too small, repeat the procedure until you get it right.

8. If you'd like to add a small border around the image, double-click the image layer and select "Stroke." Double-click the Stroke layer and set the size to 3, or whatever you like. Select an outside (exterior) or inside (interior) position, choose your color, and hit OK.

Screenshot #12

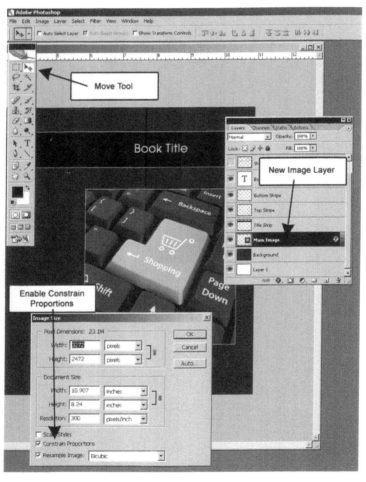

Screenshot #13

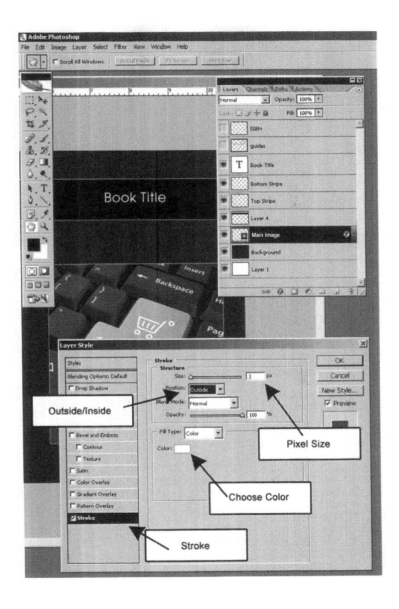

Step Six

Now we will add color to the spine area. This is optional;
you can leave it the same color if you like.

1. Add a new layer and assign it a title. Make sure this
layer is placed above the layer containing the color
strip for the title background.

2. Use the color picker to choose a color.

3. Turn on your guides layer.

4. Make sure the proper layer is selected, then use the
rectangle tool to outline the spine area.

5. Use the color picker to choose a color.

6. Fill the layer with the chosen color:
"Edit/Fill/Foreground Color."

Screenshot #14

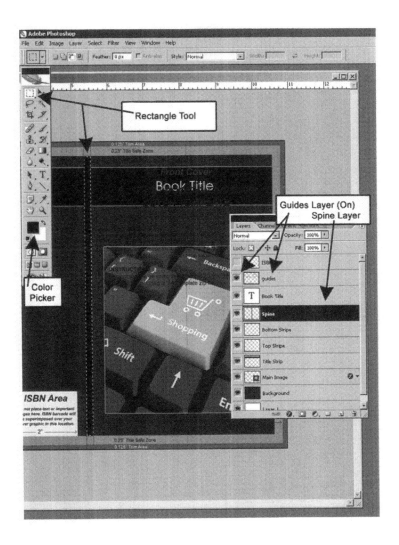

Step Seven

It's time to add content to the back cover. Keep in mind that the lower-right area of the back cover is where the ISBN number and barcode information will be displayed. Also, in this case, we will add the color strip to the back cover.

1. Turn on your guides layer and note the area you have to work with.

2. Compose the backcover text elsewhere, edit thoroughly, then paste it into a new text layer. This text typically includes a description of the book and a brief author bio.

3. Consider adding a quote or an excerpt from the book. Look at other books for tips.

4. Consider adding an image. Follow the previous instructions for adding text and images, and position them as you like. Experiment. Let the artist in you emerge.

Screenshot #15

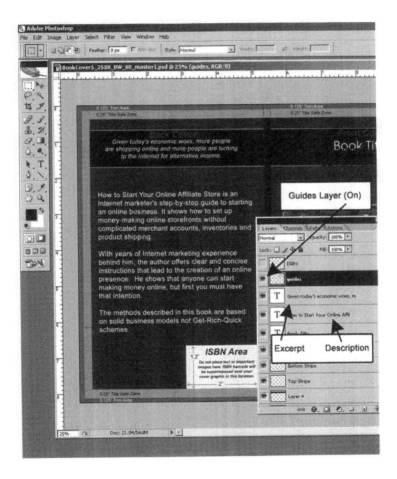

Step Eight

With the guides layer turned on, check that no content is spilling over into the trim area.

Next—and this is important—turn off the guides layer. If you leave it on, it will print out along with the other design elements.

Now we are ready to prepare the file that will be uploaded as a PDF file for CreateSpace.

1. Flatten the layers at "Layer/Flatten Image/Discard Hidden Layers." This will help reduce the final file size.

2. Save the file: "File/Save As/File Format." (Choose PDF)

3. In the first Dialogue Box, click OK.

4. In the second Dialogue Box, accept all default settings except for Compression. Under the Compression setting, set a) Compression to JPEG and b) Image Quality to High. We want the cover to have the highest quality for print.

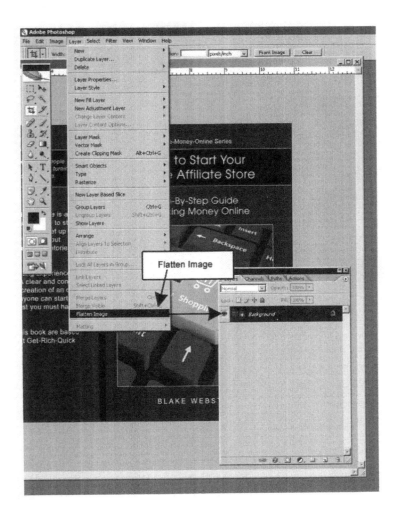

Screenshot #17

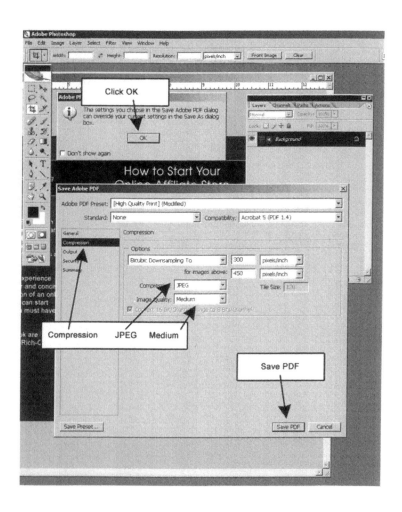

You now have a cover file ready for upload.

Section XI: Conclusion

Why Write a Book?

If you've lived a little, you've probably thought, "I should write a book." You've been to war or traveled the world; you have specialized knowledge or a great storyline. Perhaps people have told you just that: "You should write a book."

Until recently, chances were low that you'd take that advice. If you're still hesitating today, in this age of POD, maybe it's because your are unaware of how much easier book publishing has become.

Not too many years ago, if you wanted to get into print, you had a choice of two paths: 1) Solicit an agent, who would then try to persuade an editor to publish your book, an effort that, even if successful, can take years; 2) self-publish by investing thousands of dollars for thousands of books that you may or may not sell.

In other words, you either had to invest lots of time or lots of money, or both.

No longer.

Thanks first to POD and second to CreateSpace, you can now self-publish your book at virtually no cost, without an agent, and without intrusive editors demanding "fixes" you disagree with. You are the boss of you.

What's more, the sheer act of writing a book carries with it countless benefits that have nothing to do with getting published or selling books. For example:

- *It's stimulating.* Research shows that engaging in stimulating activities slows mental aging. Mental exercise can help your brain function at a higher level than it would otherwise. If thirty minutes on the treadmill each day is good for your body, imagine how thirty or more minutes a day wrestling with your words benefits the brain.

- *It's healing.* Most self-published books are nonfiction, and many are memoirs or autobiographies. By working through the pain of life, writers can find understanding and comfort.

- *It's creative.* Creativity is the route to self discovery and authenticity. As you create, you plumb the depths of your being, accessing what you think and believe. You may be surprised by what you discover.

- *It's connective.* Doing research and writing stories, especially your life stories, will help you reconnect with people.

- *It's educational.* Even when writing about your own life, you have to do research. You will learn things about yourself, your family, and the world.

- *It's purposeful.* Writing, editing, researching, publishing, and promoting a book will give you a goal for months or years. Then you can do another.

- *It's gratifying.* You will swell with pride each time you finish a chapter. You will positively balloon up when you finish a book.

- *It's liberating.* You can sing, shout, or swear from the rooftops, especially in your early drafts. Find your voice and feel the freedom in that.

- *It improves recall.* Studies show that improving our ability to process language tends to improve our recall.

- *It preserves thoughts and memories.* If not written down, they die with their owners.

- *It's a gift.* Naomi, a student in Steve's memoir-writing class, decided at age 90 to profile her family members, a tribute to their lives. When she finished, she said with satisfaction, "Now that's what I wanted to do. It's like leaving a gift for my family."

- *It's fun.*

Why Write Nonfiction?

Despite all the attention and accolades heaped upon novelists such as John Irving and Stephen King, most books sold are nonfiction. What's more, if your name is unknown to the world at large, trying to sell a first novel is akin to building a road with a butter knife. So start with nonfiction—and write the Great American Novel later, sometime when you don't care if you make money.

Besides greater average financial rewards, writing nonfiction books offers other advantages. Nonfiction lets you:

- *Learn through research.* Although you should generally write about what you know, you'll have to do research even if you're an expert. When Steve wrote Camping and Backpacking with Children, he'd been backpacking for forty years, but he still had to do extensive research on everything from sleeping bag lofts to the latest in freeze-dried foods. Even if you're not an expert when you begin your book project, you will be when you finish. And that's fun.

- *Provide instruction to others.* How-to and self-help books sell. What do you do and what do you know? What stirs your soul? Is it skeet shooting? Butterfly collecting? Baseball trivia? Teach others about it.

- *Pursue a hobby.* Is your passion scrapbooking? Do you build ships in bottles or craft giant redwood sculptures with a chainsaw? Share your tips and insights with other hobbyists.

- *Share a passion with others.* Are you angry about the state of the world? Does Man's inhumanity to Man have you muttering to yourself? Write about it. At the other end of the emotional spectrum, what fills you with joy? Is it community gardens? Organizing school fundraisers? Lay out the steps for others and make them feel your passion.

- *Inspire others to action.* People are forever seeking inspiration, and some find it in books. Think of yours as a call to action. You are, after all, trying to persuade the reader to do something—start a nonprofit, take up topiary. And when you find out that your book changed someone's life in a positive way, you will once again swell with pride.

- *Share your expertise.* Although you may have areas of specialized knowledge or experience that qualify you to write a book, all of us have at least one unique area of expertise—our own lives. Even when others are around, our perspective is unique. No one can tell your story except you.

In Final Praise of Memoir

"Write what you know," we are told. In other words, don't write about Paris fashion unless you've been there and seen it from the inside. Don't write about the sins of the Hollywood film industry unless you know that world well.

Therein lies the beauty of memoir. You are tackling a subject in which you are an expert—your life. Even if thousands of others were alongside you at Pearl Harbor or the Obama inauguration, yours is a singular viewpoint. No one else saw that day—or any other day—as you did. No one else can tell your story.

Can you feel the power in that?

Section XII: Professional Services

Web Development Services

Blake Webster is president of Media Design Services Inc., a web and multimedia company specializing in website development, Internet marketing, and search engine optimization services. For pricing and information regarding customized web services, contact Media Design Services, Inc.

More information regarding search engine optimization services can be found at
Basic SEO Direct: www.basicseodirect.com

Media Design Services Inc.
P.O. Box 3153
Santa Rosa, CA 95402
707-836-8389

Email: blake@mediadesign-mds.com

Writing, Editing, and Consulting Services

Steve Boga has authored more than 35 books and dozens of magazine articles. For the past 13 years, he has taught writing at Santa Rosa Junior College and served as editor, ghostwriter, or consultant for countless writers and writer wannabes.

If you have an idea you'd like to turn into a manuscript or a manuscript you'd like to turn into a book, contact him for a free telephone consultation.

Telephone: 707-869-1515

Email: lifestories@memoirwritings.com

Made in the USA
Lexington, KY
11 December 2010